DATAPROOF YOUR SCHOOL

HOW TO USE ASSESSMENT DATA EFFECTIVELY

James:
Katy, there are not enough words. This book is for you.

Richard:
Lindsay, none of this would be here if it wasn't for you.

DATAPROOF YOUR SCHOOL

HOW TO USE ASSESSMENT DATA EFFECTIVELY

RICHARD SELFRIDGE
JAMES PEMBROKE

CORWIN

SAGE Publications Ltd
1 Oliver's Yard
55 City Road
London EC1Y 1SP

CORWIN
A SAGE company
2455 Teller Road
Thousand Oaks, California 91320
(0800)233-9936
www.corwin.com

SAGE Publications India Pvt Ltd
B 1/I 1 Mohan Cooperative Industrial Area
Mathura Road
New Delhi 110 044

SAGE Publications Asia-Pacific Pte Ltd
3 Church Street
#10-04 Samsung Hub
Singapore 049483

Editor: James Clark
Senior assistant editor: Diana Alves
Production editor: Katherine Haw
Copyeditor: Clare Weaver
Proofreader: Leigh C. Smithson
Indexer: Elske Janssen
Cover design: Sheila Tong
Typeset by: KnowledgeWorks Global Ltd
Printed in the UK

© Richard Selfridge and James Pembroke 2022

First published 2022

Library of Congress Control Number: 2021940331

British Library Cataloguing in Publication data

A catalogue record for this book is available from the British Library

ISBN 978-1-5297-3035-7
ISBN 978-1-5297-3034-0 (pbk)

At SAGE we take sustainability seriously. Most of our products are printed in the UK using responsibly sourced papers and boards. When we print overseas we ensure sustainable papers are used as measured by the PREPS grading system. We undertake an annual audit to monitor our sustainability.

Contents

About the Authors   *vi*

Acknowledgements   *viii*

1   An Introduction to Using Data in School   1

2   A Licence to Change   15

3   Generating and Collating High-Quality Data   31

4   Standardised Tests   47

5   Teacher Assessment   69

6   Outliers   87

7   Tracking Systems   111

8   Developing a Data Strategy   135

9   Dataproofing in Action   149

Index   173

ABOUT THE AUTHORS

Richard Selfridge is a primary school teacher, data consultant and writer on education. His 2018 book for SAGE Publications, *Databusting for Schools*, is an essential guide to the use and interpretation of education data. As well as teaching, working with schools on their use of education data and writing about education, Richard works as a consultant for the Driver Youth Trust supporting inclusion for literacy. A passionate advocate of sensible use of data in schools, Richard was part of ASCL's primary assessment expert panel alongside James, which indirectly lead to James and Richard working together as the Databusters, running workshops across the country and co-hosting the Databusters podcast. In his spare time, Richard can be found hunting follies, usually by bike, or playing, listening to, watching, talking or thinking about music. He lives in Leeds with his wife Lindsay and daughters Martha and Connie.

James Pembroke has 15 years' experience of working with education data, including five years working as a data analyst in a local authority school improvement team. He set up the Sig+ consultancy in 2014 to help schools across the country make sense of their data and has been tweeting, blogging and talking on the subject ever since. James has worked with many organisations – notably as a member of ASCL's primary assessment expert panel and the Department for Education's Reception Baseline Stakeholder Group – and has spoken at numerous national conferences including the legendary Learning First events. He joined the team at Insight in 2018 where he continues to fight against zombie levels and advise schools on the rights and wrongs of tracking. When he's not working with data, James goes bouldering and runs up and down hills. He lives in Cheltenham with his wife Katy and daughters Martha and Rosa.

ACKNOWLEDGEMENTS

So many people have inspired us to write this book. We are particularly grateful to Andrew Percival, Natalie Jackson and Steve Ellis for their valued contributions. Thanks also to Diana Alves at SAGE for your patience and support throughout this project, and for gifting us a wonderful opportunity. To Andrew and Sarah at Insight, thank you for all your encouragement and for building such a great system. Thanks to the following, whose advice and writing has helped shape our ideas: Mary Myatt, Nancy Gedge, Ruth Swailes, Ben Newmark, Rob Coe, Becky Allen and everyone else who have shared their thoughts on how to dataproof their schools with us. Thanks also to all those who attended our 2019–20 Databusters workshops and listened to us think out loud as we honed the ideas we have distilled into these pages. And finally, thank you to the hundreds of hardworking and brilliant teachers we have spoken to over the years. Those countless conversations – your experiences and ideas – have coalesced into the thoughts contained in this book and it would never have happened without you.

AN INTRODUCTION TO USING DATA IN SCHOOL

1.1   An introduction to using data in school

Schools are awash with data and every day adds more to the pile. Teachers generate data on their classes in every lesson. School leaders are asked to gather, collate and analyse data in their quest to improve the education on offer to children in their schools and report to governors. At school network level, those responsible for wider networks of schools are also tasked with using data generated to drive school improvement. Ostensibly, school data is gathered for the purposes of improving outcomes for pupils. But does it always fulfil this fundamental aim? It is an inconvenient truth that not all data provides useful information.

The sheer amount of data available in schools can be overwhelming and the process of gathering it can often become an end in itself. What's more, much of the analysis of data in school is questionable and, in many cases, does little to drive what actually happens in the classroom. Sadly, it is not uncommon for school data to stray into realms of fantasy, where undue credibility is given to abstract numbers that are utterly disconnected from the reality of assessment.

In this book, we seek to change this narrative. We want schools to re-focus the use of the data they generate to support the teaching and learning which happens at classroom level.

Dataproof Your School does this in the light of what we now know about teaching, learning and the business of education in schools. It also takes into account the regulatory frameworks in which schools have been operating, and the avenues down which many have been driven by those seeking to hold schools to account.

We also recognise that, whilst those who lead schools are frequently interested in the intricacies and history of school data development, most of those people tasked with running schools are busy and want simply to know what they should do to harness and use their data effectively. This book will therefore act as a roadmap to help schools develop a viable data strategy that is sustainable, effective and has buy-in from all staff.

Box 1.1 — Working out what works in education

After over a hundred years of compulsory education, substantial investment in education as a nation and the collation of enormous amounts of data on schools and the students in them, surely we should know where to direct our efforts to improve outcomes in schools? When Michael Gove moved into the Department for Education (DfE) in 2010, he began the process of publishing much of the data collected by the department – an additional 14 million items of exam data in 2011 alone (DfE, 2011). Huge amounts of information were made available for educational researchers to investigate what actually happens in the education system. The Education Endowment Foundation (EEF), which publishes a Teaching and Learning Toolkit designed to summarise educational research, was set up to undertake and share educational research (Selfridge, 2018: 223–4).

England is not alone in its data generation and focus on researching 'what works'. The US government-funded Institute for Education Studies runs the What Works Clearinghouse, which summarises research and publishes practice guides for those in school.

In addition, there are thousands of researchers across the world who examine a multitude of different areas of education, from using technology to supporting teachers' professional development, from innovative classroom practice to tried and tested programmes which have been used in schools for decades.

So, what does work? In summary, there are a small number of things which schools should probably do, and a large number for which there is little or no evidence of effectiveness. The EEF's initial guide to literacy at Key Stage 2, for example, lists seven areas in three broad categories which it suggests schools should probably do.

Whilst the EEF's focus is on supporting those children who are disadvantaged compared to the national average, their findings are quite stark: there are very few, if any, magic bullets which can help children to make accelerated progress compared to their peers. The EEF's 'Guide to the Pupil Premium' (EEF, 2019: 4) (the additional financial support given to schools for each child held to be economically disadvantaged) suggests that there are three main areas on which schools should concentrate:

1. Improving teaching
2. Targeted academic support
3. Wider strategies

Improving teaching simply means making sure that existing teachers are given high-quality opportunities for professional development, particularly in the early years of

(Continued)

teaching. Targeted academic support simply means that additional support should be evidence-informed and well structured. Wider strategies simply mean supporting children and families to ensure that pupils are in school, in class and able to focus on learning.

In essence, what the extensive body of research into teaching, learning and schooling suggests is that it is important to ensure that teachers are well supported and that pupils are in school, in class, focused and learning what we want them to.

We bring two different but related perspectives to the issue of data use in schools. Richard began his career in education as a primary school teacher. James began working with education data as a data analyst for a local authority. Both of us have come to the view that all too often the way in which schools use data is, at best, an uncomfortable compromise and, at worst, a huge drain on over-extended resources.

We believe that schools can, and should, do better.

In the early 2010s, in his role as a classroom teacher, Richard began to question some of the ways schools were being judged based on data. With a background in statistics, he realised that many of those working in and with schools were not in a position to challenge much of the orthodoxy which had arisen surrounding assessment data in particular. Additionally, much of the information which schools could be using was not being utilised effectively because the accountability frameworks put in place often encouraged short-termism and did not improve the quality of education in schools.

Richard eventually wrote a book, *Databusting for Schools* (2018), which included a history of data as used in schools and explored the underlying statistics which have been applied to school data. Whilst many readers have clearly found the book useful, and have used it to help them think about the way they use data in school, a common response has been to ask for a simple, easy-to-follow guide to what schools should do with their data.

James came to education data as an analyst, working initially with government datasets but increasingly advising schools on effective use of data and helping companies develop tools capable of collating and analysing school data in all its forms.

Over the past five years, since leaving his data analyst role in a local authority school improvement team, James has come to realise that certain 'truths' around school data, particularly in the murky world of tracking pupil progress, are at best flawed, and often completely false. And yet, schools still devote inordinate amounts of staff time in pursuit of such measures in the illusion that they are meaningful, necessary or both. Such distractions are obviously things that busy schools can do without.

Thankfully, the government's removal of levels in 2014 lifted the lid on the problems with assessment data and started a national conversation about what works. This, combined with Ofsted's shift in position with regards to data, has given schools licence to move their data in the right direction without fear of repercussions. Everyone involved in education now needs to grasp this.

Both of us are school governors, and we have extensive experience working with governors and school leaders on interpreting and guiding development of summaries of school data for governors. Whilst governors need to understand the data available to them, they also need to accept that data should not be generated solely for their benefit. They should also provide constructive challenge to school leadership teams on the validity of data presented to them as well as question its workload implications.

In the work we have done both separately and together – we have been running 'Databusting' seminars across the country based on the ideas contained in this book – we hear a common refrain from teachers, school leaders and governors: What do we need to know about school data? And what should we do to ensure that we make the most of it?

1.2   What should teachers and school leaders want to know?

We believe that the fundamental question schools should ask is this: What do we want to know and how will this knowledge help us to make a difference to the education we provide within school?

These are markedly different questions to those that are often asked: What data do we have to collect? What do we need to prove that we are a good – or better – school? Such questions are a reaction to the external demands made of schools. And whilst some schools have moved beyond this accountability-focused framework, many are beginning to realise that the way they have used data up until now has been reactive rather than proactive. We want schools to take back control of their data by asking some foundational questions.

Box 1.2   **What does 'data' mean in most schools at the moment?**

In 2020, the Fischer Family Trust (FFT) Datalab published *How is data used in schools today?*, a research report which utilised data gathered by Teacher Tapp, an innovative research tool developed by Professor Becky Allen and Laura McInerney. This followed the initial report published in 2019, which provided fascinating insight into the situation in England's schools.

The vast majority of schools ask their teaching teams to gather and submit attainment data at least once a term, with over 90% of schools providing data termly and almost 50% doing so half-termly. Whilst some schools submit data weekly, fortnightly or twice a year, they were in vanishingly small minorities.

(Continued)

This collation of data is likely to be a hangover of the requirement (introduced in the 2000s) for schools to submit data to central government summarising current and likely future attainment of pupils, a process generally known as target setting. The Department for Education was mandated by law to require schools to generate, gather, collate and submit this type of data until the early 2010s.

In 2020, nine in ten schools collated data into a tracking system of some sort, with two-thirds of these systems being externally purchased systems provided by commercial companies. The data being entered onto these systems was largely assessment made by teachers, with around 20% of schools using externally created assessments derived from standardised tests in addition to or as a replacement for teacher assessment.

Just under 50% of primary teachers were asked to track over 50 pupil standards or objectives over a school year. Secondary school teachers reported that their schools were largely using GCSE standards to measure attainment and progress in Key Stage 3 and Key Stage 4 with a third or more using likely future grades based on current attainment. More primary than secondary schools were using standardised scores, although at 20% (compared to less than 10% in secondary schools) these were still rare.

One in five headteachers – and 54% of classroom teachers – reported that they would like to collect data less frequently. Almost 70% of teachers felt that the analysis of pupil assessment data was somewhat or very important for improving education outcomes for pupils.

The Teacher Tapp panel were split in their view as to whether they had too much or the right amount of data and information, with slightly more teachers reporting that they had about the right amount to make informed decisions in their job role.

Whilst the Teacher Tapp data is extremely useful as an insight into the data schools gather for their own use, this is not the only data that schools generate. Governments across the world have become increasingly interested in pupil attainment, and in how this changes over time. As a result, schools are frequently asked to assess or test pupils and to submit the resultant data to central government.

In England, schools are required to generate, collate and submit attainment data for pupils in the school year in which they turn 11 (Year 6), 16 (Year 11) and 18 (Year 13). Year 6 pupils sit SATs in Mathematics, Reading, and Spelling, Punctuation and Grammar (SPAG). Year 11 pupils take a variety of assessments including GCSEs (General Certificate of Secondary Education), BTECs (Business and Technology Education Council qualifications) and NVQs (National Vocational Qualifications). Year 13 pupils take assessments including A Levels, BTECs (Business and Technology Education Council qualifications) and NVQs (National Vocational Qualifications).

Additionally, teachers of pupils in Year 6 are required to make judgements in Writing based on pupils' work in class. Teachers of pupils in Year 2 (the year children turn 7) are required to make statutory judgements in Mathematics, Reading, and Writing, which acts as both an attainment marker at that point and a baseline for progress measures at Key Stage 2. At the time of writing, a new baseline assessment was due to be implemented in autumn 2021, assessing pupils entering the reception year (the year pupils turn 5 years of age). This assessment will provide the baseline for Key Stage 2 progress measures in future and its roll out will enable the Department for Education to scrap Key Stage 1 assessment in 2023. Primary schools are also mandated to undertake the profile assessment at the end of the Early Years Foundation Stage (the end of reception year), the Phonics Screening Check in Year 1, and a Multiplication Tables Check in Year 4.

This statutory data is analysed by central government and further statistics are generated, becoming part of what is often grouped together as 'school data'. Such data provides two functions: it enables the government to track attainment of national cohorts over time to assess the impact of reforms, and it provides teachers with an in-depth prior attainment history for their pupils.

So, what do we want to know? Broadly, we can separate data into four categories: context (personal details that may affect learning); attainment (results of assessments including statutory assessments); development (the progress a pupil is making, their effort and attitude to learning); and provision (strategies put in place to support pupils' learning).

Fundamentally, we want to know where the challenges are, how pupils develop over time, where to focus our efforts, and whether or not our efforts are effective.

1.2.1 Where are the challenges?

As discussed in the 'Working out what works in education' box above, in order for children to get the most out of their time in school, they need to be in school, in class, focused on learning and learning the things we want them to.

For some children and some schools, ensuring that children are actually on site is a key challenge. Schools have been encouraged to focus on attendance, with data for both overall and persistent absence being key performance indicators. We discuss this in Chapter 3. In summary, children cannot learn if they are not in school and the effect of gaps in attendance can persist throughout a child's education. We need to know if a child has not attended school and we need to know why they have been absent.

For some children, the challenge is to ensure that they are in class. The majority of schools have systems to manage children's education if they are not able to learn in class with their peers. A minority of children have behaviour difficulties which mean that they may be removed from class; whilst schools often plan for learning during these episodes, any time spent out of class as a result of a child's behaviour in the classroom is a challenge. Whilst some children may be out of class due to behaviour that disrupts the learning of others, others may be educated elsewhere for periods of time for other reasons. We look at the issues which arise in Chapter 6.

For some children, the challenge comes within the classroom. Children have considerable agency, in that their attitude to learning and school affects their learning. Whilst schools have a significant role in shaping children's focus, some children need support to ensure that they are actually focusing on learning what their teachers want them to. We discuss this challenge in Chapter 3.

If children are in school, in class and focused on learning, the challenge is then to ensure that children are actually learning what has been planned for them to learn. The effective assessment of attainment and development over time is the core of this book, and we look at assessment of written work, reading, mathematics and the wider curriculum in Chapters 4, 5 and 6.

1.2.2 Development over time

We have deliberately steered away from using the word 'progress' at this point. We will make an effort to reclaim this word later in this book, but for now we will use the phrase 'development over time'. In short, whilst the purpose of education is somewhat disputed, one core purpose is to ensure that children are able to learn the things we want them to during their time in school.

We know that children develop physically, emotionally and intellectually over time. English education is split into Early Years and five Key Stages; countries across the world expect children of different ages and stages to learn what is deemed appropriate via age-appropriate curriculums.

We want to know whether children have developed over time; more particularly, we want to know whether children have not made the development we might have expected. If they have not, we want to be able to support them to catch up, where possible. If children have not made typical development, data can provide crucial insight into ways schools might respond.

Where children have made accelerated progress compared to their peers, we need to use the data we have to help us to understand the implications this may have for the child, their classes and their schools, both now and during their remaining time in our care.

We discuss outliers in Chapter 6, looking at what schools should do to support those who are at the extremes of the typical distribution of children within school.

In Chapter 8, we will outline the development of a school data strategy; this will provide a step-by-step guide to help you to take control of your data so you can dataproof your school.

1.2.3 Where to focus effort

Schools have limited resources, whether this be money, effort or time. What's more, as Dylan Wiliam often notes, 'Everything works somewhere and nothing works everywhere' (Wiliam, 2018: 2). And, as Becky Allen and Sam Sims (2018: 52) add, 'Thousands of schools, operating seemingly independently, have chosen to embark on a similar set of bureaucratic activities that were never mandated and cannot be explained by any sort of efficiency drive to improve pupil learning'. In short, schools could – if they chose – try to do everything, even though many things will not actually make much difference. Much of what schools do is done because other schools do something similar.

There are many reasons why schools do follow the pack. Those on the edges are often targeted by wolves, after all. Many working in schools have become wary of external accountability frameworks which have encouraged inefficient and questionable practices, and accountability has become the main driving force behind data collection in many settings.

Changes to the accountability framework do seem to reflect concerns raised by many of us working in the school system. The 2019 Education Inspection Framework includes a great deal to reassure schools that practices which result in excess workload are not mandated in any way. Moreover, Ofsted's *School Inspection Handbook* (DfE, 2021: 214) contains the explicit warning that 'If a school's system for data collection is disproportionate, inefficient or unsustainable for staff, inspectors will reflect this in their reporting on the school'.

This, then, presents a clear opportunity for schools. Rather than creating and storing data for others – for those external agencies that scrutinise school performance, for example – we now have the freedom to develop more appropriate, meaningful approaches. We recommend that schools consider their context and direct their efforts accordingly. Where attendance is an issue for some pupils, focus on that. Where presence in class is an issue, place your focus there. Where some pupils are not engaged in their learning, focus on this. Where there are pupils who are not learning what we want them to despite your best efforts, place your focus on finding ways to support those individuals. There is no one-size-fits-all approach: the information you require for one pupil will differ from that required for another. In terms of learning, some pupils are fine and some are not. It is the latter group for whom you will require more in-depth and diverse data.

Box 1.3	What data do you generate, collate and analyse?

Take a moment to consider what data is generated within your school or schools. What are teachers expected to generate, collate and analyse? What information is collated centrally by administrative staff, and how is this analysed?

(Continued)

How robust is the data which is held centrally? How often is the data refreshed, and what is the scope of your data? Consider the following questions:

- What information do you hold regarding pupils?
- How does pupil data develop over time?
- How often do you collect attainment data?
- How do you store data?
- How do you analyse data?
- How useful do you find the data you hold?
- What data might you prefer to gather, collate and analyse?
- Would there be an adverse impact on learning if you stopped collecting certain data?

1.3   Thinking strategically about data

Schools generally work within a policy framework, in which protocols or procedures are established and followed to ensure consistency in decision making. Policies have their place, but to dataproof your school, we want you to make changes over time so that the way in which you use data will be different in future. To do this, you will need to think strategically; to plan for a different future.

Thinking strategically will enable you to make changes over time which will result in improved use of data at all levels. By setting goals, deciding how you will achieve them, and directing effort to make the adjustments which are deemed necessary, you will be able to ensure that you begin to control your data rather than being controlled by it.

A Data Strategy will help to focus your efforts by clarifying the strengths, weaknesses, opportunities and threats of your school's generation, collation, analysis and use of data. Thinking strategically will allow you to make the changes you want in a gradual, manageable and sustainable process over time. By taking time to consider and evaluate the nature and purpose of data, schools can move from an accountability-driven system towards an approach more focused on learning and support.

We will explore this in detail in Chapter 8, as we help you to develop a dynamic data strategy that will enable you to take control of the use of data in your school.

Rather than starting by launching straight into what you might do, you will be guided to consider why and how you will take control of the information systems in your school. Once you have a clear rationale for using data to drive school improvement, and an understanding of the difference between your current position and where you would like to be, you will be in a strong position to develop the data strategy you need in order to implement the changes you are going to make.

1.4   Dataproof your school

The need to dataproof your school has never been greater. As schools are becoming increasingly autonomous – within a regulatory framework that expects schools to make decisions locally rather than to follow central diktats – there is an increased expectation that schools will make decisions that benefit the families, communities and pupils they exist to support. Additionally, schools are expected to ensure that those working within them are working effectively and efficiently, focusing on maximising impact to ensure children are given the best possible opportunity to learn.

The workload impact of ineffective and inefficient data management in schools is a high priority for the government. The Department for Education's Workload Reduction Toolkit (DfE, 2018) places it first in its list of areas for schools to focus on when considering workload issues. Over 70% of teachers in both primary and secondary reported that they spent 'too much time' on data management in the 2016 Teacher Workload Survey (DfE, 2017); 60% of secondary school teachers continued to report that they spent too much time on data management, as did over half of primary school teachers (DfE, 2019).

In a dataproof school, the gathering and collating of data is kept to a minimum whilst providing all of the information necessary to identify the ongoing challenges for individual pupils, their classes and their cohorts on which schools need to focus.

As we both know from our work in and with schools, knowledge about the benefits and limitations of pupil performance data is – for a wide variety of reasons – often limited within the teaching profession. Without a detailed understanding of the benefits and limitations of pupil data, schools often struggle to get the balance of data management right at classroom level, as the DfE data above demonstrates. Consequently, collection of data, implementation of tracking systems and employment of standardised tests can often be a kneejerk reaction to the pressures of accountability, perhaps copying what other schools are doing or adopting the recommendations of external advisors.

Changes in the assessments mandated by central government have left many teachers and school leaders struggling, uncertain as to what and how to assess in school. The move away from teacher assessment towards greater use of standardised tests, particularly in primary schools, has brought many challenges, as has the removal of coursework elements of secondary qualifications.

In Chapter 3, we look at the essential tools that schools should use to take control of their data. This will focus on data-management systems, and the contextual, attainment and development data, as well as statutory data that schools hold. Contextual data includes information such as pupils' age, particularly within their cohort, their medical and developmental attendance and educational mobility and stability, and other important factors relating to special educational needs and disability (SEND), language and deprivation. Tracking and building up a picture over time is essential to ensure that each pupil, class and cohort within your school is given the support they need.

Attainment data is vital to ensure that pupils' development – especially when compared to earlier cohorts and national reference groups – is tracked over time; and statutory attainment data adds a great deal of useful information to a school's dataset. Whilst attainment data has many problematic aspects – particularly when what might be inferred from it is poorly understood, or simply wrong – an in-depth knowledge of such assessments is vital: cautious and sensible use of standardised assessments is essential in a dataproof school.

Our focus is also on helping schools to best direct their efforts when it comes to ensuring that the gathering, collation and analysis of data at a school-wide level has effective and lasting impact. Too often, in our experience, schools collect data as an end in itself. Equally, too often, data is needlessly limited and does not build over time.

Any data gathered and collated centrally should – following intelligent analysis and summation – lead to actions for pupils, classes and cohorts. Often, the action will be to continue to teach the curriculum as it stands. At times, the action should be to amend the curriculum for limited periods or on an ongoing basis. For some individuals and groups, or for some classes, the action will be to put in place specific targeted support. In all cases, data should lead to action.

A dataproof school is one in which everyone is aware how and why information is gathered, and what actions are put in place as a result for those in their charge. Effort is proportionate, the focus is on impact and, at all times, the data supports dynamic and decisive decision making.

1.5   How to use this book

We will guide you through the process of becoming a dataproof school, starting with a chapter outlining current schools' landscape. In Chapter 3, we look at the need to ensure that your data is of a high quality, before looking at standardised tests in Chapter 4 and teacher assessments in Chapter 5.

Data is crucial in identifying and supporting outliers within school. Chapter 6 explores this in some detail, looking at the most common groups of pupils in schools who, in most cases, need additional support or monitoring when compared to their peers. Much of the action arising from the analysis of data within a dataproof school will relate to pupils who are – for whatever reason – clearly on the edges of a normal distribution of pupils.

We look at keeping track of your data in Chapter 7, and in Chapter 8, we will help you to develop a clear strategy for the gathering, analysis and use of pupil data. We will guide you through the process of deciding what data are important to meet the needs of parents, teachers, school leaders, governors and administration staff in the short, medium and longer term.

In Chapter 9, we look at dataproofing in action. Through all of this we will weave case studies, continuing professional development opportunities and points for you to consider as you progress towards dataproofing your school.

References

Allen, R. and Sims, S. (2018) *The Teacher Gap*. Oxford: Routledge.

Department for Education (DfE) (2011) *Michael Gove on the Moral Purpose of School Reform*. London: DfE.

Department for Education (DfE) (2017) *Teacher Workload Survey 2016*. London: DfE.

Department for Education (DfE) (2018) *Workload Reduction Toolkit*. London: DfE.

Department for Education (DfE) (2019) *Teacher Workload Survey 2019*. London: DfE.

Department for Education (DfE) (2021) *School Inspection Handbook*. London: DfE.

Education Endowment Foundation (EEF) (2019) *Guide to the Pupil Premium*. London: EEF.

Fischer Family Trust (FFT) (2020) *How is Data Used in School Today?* London: FFT.

Selfridge, R. (2018) *Databusting for Schools*. London: Sage Publications.

Wiliam, D. (2018) *Creating the School Our Pupils Need*. West Palm Beach: Learning Science International.

A LICENCE TO CHANGE

2.1 The purpose of data in schools

Why do schools collect data? This is the fundamental question that lies at the heart of this book. Is a school's approach to data focused on learning, on providing teachers with useful information to support the pupils in their classrooms? Or is it driven by a desire, expectation or requirement to prove something to those with oversight, both within and outside of the school?

If a school's data strategy is a wheel, what is the hub upon which it is built?

It is understandable that schools want to use data as evidence of performance. Teachers report to senior leaders, senior leaders report to the headteacher, the headteacher reports to governors and external agencies. There is a chain of command and each link may be expected to report up, to show that progress is being made. Certainly, with government measures based on the results of national assessments carried out in reception (Early Years Foundation Stage Profile), Year 1 (phonics), Year 2 (Key Stage 1), Year 4 (multiplication tables check), Year 6 (Key Stage 2 tests), Year 11 (GCSE) and Year 13 (A Levels), accountability is inescapable. The government has a vast amount of data with which to measure, rank and compare schools over time, and this data is forged into a plethora of attainment and progress metrics that are published in various formats for various audiences. Some is aimed at schools and governors, ostensibly for the purposes of school improvement. Some data is generated for Ofsted (England's school inspectorate) to identify strengths and weaknesses and to prioritise the order of inspection, targeting schools deemed most at risk. Finally, there is the data in the public domain, intended for parents to help them make choices about schools for their children.

The focus of these statutory assessments is clear: accountability – to measure school performance, to rank schools in order, to inform key audiences of schools that are succeeding and those that are failing. The use of data in this way is perhaps inevitable. The problem with using statutory assessment this way is that it applies stress to the system; and the result of stress is strain. When strain goes beyond a certain point in a physical system it results in deformation of material. Assessment and its resultant data are no different: they get bent out of shape by the forces acting upon them. We now have a clear risk to the integrity of assessment data; not just the statutory, national assessments, but also to the ongoing assessment system the school should be employing to support pupils' learning. The focus shifts away from the classroom towards satisfying the demands of those with a school improvement remit. The problem is that there is now a temptation to provide a rose-tinted view of goings on, rather than the warts and all picture that all concerned so desperately need.

The irony is that accountability can distort the very evidence that it relies upon to be effective.

This leads to some difficult but necessary conversations about types of data, styles of assessment and the conditions under which assessment is carried out. National tests at Key Stages 2, 4 and 5 are heavily regulated, and as such are generally reliable (although still susceptible to maladministration). Other assessments, particularly those in primary schools, are far more dependent on teachers' judgements which are, by their nature, more subjective and prone to distortion.

As stated above, these risks are not limited to statutory assessment; they can affect assessments in all forms at any point where that assessment is used to generate data that is then used to monitor school and staff performance.

Over the past few years, there have been a number of key reports that have warned schools of the risks of data distortion. Notably, many of these reports have been endorsed and published by the Department for Education.

The final report of the Commission on Assessment without Levels warned that:

> some types of assessment are capable of being used for more than one purpose. However, this may distort the results, such as where an assessment is used to monitor pupil performance but is also used as evidence for staff performance management. School leaders should be careful to ensure that the primary purpose of assessment is not distorted by using it for multiple purposes. In-school summative assessment should not be driven by nationally collected forms of statutory summative assessment. What works best for national accountability purposes does not necessarily work best for supporting teaching and learning or for monitoring pupil progress. (Commission on Assessment without Levels, 2015)

And yet, all too often, internal assessment data is used as an indicator of results in future national tests. It is also used to monitor teacher effectiveness, to evaluate department and whole school performance, and to compare one school to another. Whilst this is perhaps difficult to avoid, we have to face the inconvenient fact that using assessment data for multiple purposes – expecting that we can use it to support learning whilst also relying on it to judge the performance of teachers and schools – risks compromising the data itself. This is a particular issue if the data in question is based on teacher – i.e. human – judgement. Even in ideal conditions, 'whilst teachers certainly know their pupils best, they are also subject – as all humans are – to bias' (Christodoulou, 2016: 105). We cannot, therefore, expect teachers to make accurate assessments if we intend to use those assessments to measure their performance as well as that of their pupils. The Education Endowment Foundation's (n.d.) *Assessing and Monitoring Pupil Progress* Toolkit makes the point:

> To improve the quality of teacher assessments it is important to consider how to […] reduce systematic biases.

Data is essential and unavoidable in schools. Data gives teachers vital information about children's characteristics, background and achievements, which builds a picture of learning as well as providing warnings of potential bumps in the road. Schools need data in order to function effectively, but they need to be aware that pressure to generate data for purposes other than supporting learning is likely to result in distortion and consequent erosion of its reliability. Let us look at some of the sources of that pressure.

2.2 External pressures

The greatest pressure exerted on schools comes from external sources. In England, this includes the government's Department for Education, the national school inspectorate (Ofsted), the regional commissioning bodies for academy schools, and local authorities. The government set statutory assessments and publish the results in league tables for all to see; regional commissioners and local authorities closely monitor school performance, and challenge and intervene in those schools that are deemed to be '*causing concern*' (DfE, 2020); and Ofsted use data as part of their risk assessment process, identifying and prioritising schools for inspection, and to provide important background information to inspectors prior to and during inspection. However, not all agencies engage with a school's internally generated data.

The Department for Education is remote and, as such, will not be scrutinising internal assessment and data processes – they are concerned solely with the results of statutory assessments. Ofsted, once heavily reliant on internal data and no doubt still exerting influence on schools in this area, have recently changed their position entirely. Realising the inherent reliability issues in much of the data they encountered, and how their engagement with such data only exacerbated those issues, they have taken the decision to disregard a school's internal data during inspections. Other agencies, however, along with numerous consultants working in the field of school improvement, are still very much interested in internal data, and schools may be required to produce data in a specified format that does not align with their assessment policy or with the systems they have in place. This is particularly the case for the 'schools causing concern' that are subject to frequent visits and obligated to submit regular data that demonstrates the progress of all cohorts and subgroups of pupils in each subject. Furthermore, there are data requirements for pupils with SEND that schools report as being obsolete yet continue to provide in order to secure funding. And in some areas, schools are requested to submit targets despite there no longer being a statutory requirement to do so.

All these factors have implications for the reliability of data as well as for teacher workload and are at odds with the recommendations of the key reports mentioned above, as well as with the 'mythbusting' statements of the Ofsted handbook. This will be dealt with in Section 2.5.

Another external group that can influence data collection in a school is parents. Schools have a statutory duty to prepare an annual report on children's achievements for parents, but there is no prescribed format to the data contained in those reports. The format needs to be accessible and informative, and schools should resist creating grades and progress scores solely meet the demands of parents. More on this in Chapter 9.

2.3   Internal pressures

The key issue here is performance management. Various groups with oversight responsibility – governors, the executive boards of multi-academy trusts, senior leadership teams – use data to track performance. There is a need to check whether standards are improving or declining, to compare to national averages or targets, and to monitor the impact of school improvement strategies. All of this is an essential part of the running of the school. The problem is it also applies stress to assessment that can result in the distortion of data.

Monitoring the performance of a school, department, or individual teachers on the basis of assessments that the teachers are responsible for and have control over is clearly a risk. We must ask ourselves: is it possible that the culture in a school could result in data being manipulated in any way? There may be a temptation to inflate assessments to provide an improved picture, and there may be a perverse incentive to lower baselines in some cases, to give the impression of greater progress.

In many primary schools, teachers are set targets for a certain percentage of pupils to reach 'age-related expectations' by the end of the year, or to make 'expected progress'. Often these targets will be met in the interim years – prior to Year 6 – giving the impression that the cohort is on track, only for final standards at Key Stage 2 to fall short of expectations. Likewise, in secondary schools, pupils may follow the prescribed flightpath only to fall short of target grades in their final exams. It is, of course, inevitable that some pupils will fall short of expectations, but we must consider the difficult prospect that data is being overestimated in order to compare favourably to performance management targets. This, of course, is counterproductive and goes against the core purpose of summative assessment: to gain a true picture of standards in a school. A possible knock-on effect of this is the setting of targets that are too low and therefore more easily achieved.

Understandably, many schools have implemented standardised tests as a way of improving the reliability of assessment. Standardised tests are extremely valuable (we will deal with them in Chapter 4) but using them for the purposes of performance management is highly problematic. Teachers, knowing that the results are viewed as a reflection of their performance, are more likely to teach these tests, which will undermine the value of the data. Moreover, conditions under which the tests are taken may be relaxed.

Schools must do whatever they can to ensure that the data they use to monitor standards is as reliable as possible. The dilemma that schools struggle with is this: you can have accurate assessment data, or you can use it for performance management. It is very difficult to have both.

Governors and executive boards have responsibility for oversight and therefore have data requirements of their own. As such, they can influence decisions taken on data collection and apply stress to the system. Ideally, a school's assessment system is designed around the needs of teachers, and the pupils in their classrooms, and primarily exists to support pupils' learning. The data supplied to internal and external audiences should be a by-product of a system designed in this way, and they should be prepared to work with the format, volume and frequency of data that the school ordinarily uses to monitor the progress of pupils.

Inevitably, preparation of data in the form of reports takes time, and this is essential as long as it presents useful information to the intended audiences and enables them to carry out their core duties of providing challenge and strategic direction.

However, many schools report that their approach to assessment, and the systems they implement, are influenced by the data that committees and boards expect or demand. The removal of levels highlighted this issue and presented schools with significant challenges, as their attempts to move towards more meaningful and proportionate methods were hampered by those who continued to expect data in a familiar format and frequency. In such cases, senior leaders readily admitted to maintaining systems, and producing data, for no other reason than to keep other people happy.

To dataproof our schools we need to reduce the pressures that risk distorting the data we rely upon to monitor standards and improve outcomes. Tackling the internal factors is the first port of call.

2.4　The problem with progress measures

In 2014, the DfE announced its intention to remove levels from the national curriculum and in doing so strip them out of the accountability system. This was a radical move. Levels were so deeply printed into the fabric of education it was perhaps inevitable that many schools would immediately seek to recreate them.

Initially designed as a broad indicator of attainment at each key stage and as a way of showing the progress pupils made between key stages, levels were removed for several reasons: they labelled pupils, provided no specific information about actual learning, promoted pace at the expense of depth, gave the illusion of consistency and comparability between subjects, influenced the curriculum that pupils were exposed to, and potentially caused the lowering of expectations by targeting specific levels at the end of the next key stage.

Many of the issues stemmed from the implication that progress was linear and the expectation that pupils should improve by a fixed number of levels between each key stage. This was challenged by an FFT Education Datalab blog post, which revealed that only one in ten pupils made the anticipated linear progress between Key Stages 1 and 4, noting wryly that:

> More children get to the 'right' place in the 'wrong' way, than get to the 'right' place in the 'right' way! (Treadaway, 2015)

And yet this expectation became a measure, and the measure became a target for every pupil in every subject in every school. An entire accountability system had been built around a myth. Goodhart's Law – often summarised as 'when a measure becomes a target, it ceases to be a good measure' – captures this perfectly.

Removing levels was supposed to be the hard reset the system needed, but progress measures are still an obsession. Quantifying the distance travelled by pupils between two points in their learning is often the main driving force behind data collection in schools, and entire systems are designed to that end.

Progress measures are a problem.

Prior to 2016, schools in England were subject to two often conflicting progress measures: valued added, which compared a pupil's result to the average result of pupils nationally with the same prior attainment; and 'expected progress', which prescribed a certain number of levels of progress that each pupil should make from their respective start points (two levels of progress between Key Stages 1 and 2; three levels of progress between Key Stages 2 and 4). Confusingly, it was entirely possible for all pupils in a school to make expected progress in terms of levels, but for the value added to be negative and even significantly below average.

Initially, levels of progress were counted across the multiple years of key stages, but schools soon came under increasing pressure to measure and 'prove' progress over shorter and shorter periods: first years, then terms, then half terms. The expectation of two levels over four years turned into one level over two years and then half a level over a year. 'Whole' levels were split into three sublevels, which worked for a while, but half a level per year, rather inconveniently, equated to one and a half sublevels and half a sublevel did not exist.

But could it?

A scoring system applied to the levels spaced each sublevel out in two-point increments. This provided schools with the capacity to divide sublevels even further into single-point units – half sublevels. Before long, teachers were discussing whether pupils were working at 3b or 3b+, and whether they had made a point of progress since the last assessment.

None of this was real, of course: no one knew the difference between 3b and a 3b+; pupils did not make a point of progress each term; the curriculum is not neatly packaged into regular-sized units of equal value gained every six weeks. These facts were overlooked in the pursuit of convenient progress measures that would satisfy internal and external demands for 'proof' that learning had happened over time. The forces exerted by the accountability system had bent assessment beyond its elastic limit and it had snapped. Something had to change.

Almost as soon as the decision to remove levels had been made, new systems emerged that looked suspiciously like the old ones; and in some cases they were the old ones, just with new names for the old sublevels. The comfort of the familiar. The earliest versions of these systems, usually involving three bands through which pupils progressed across the year, provided schools with the desired continuity of three points per year. These bands, particularly in primary settings, were given names like 'emerging, developing, secure', 'beginning, advancing, deep', or 'entering, exploring, independent', which sounded new and in keeping with the focus on mastery, but all too often such subdivisions translated as 'autumn, spring, summer'. They were linked to the percentage of the year's curriculum objectives that the pupil had secured, and these objectives were neatly packaged up into thirds, based on a simplistic assumption that schools cover 33% of the curriculum by Christmas and 67% by Easter – a system entirely at odds with curriculum design and delivery, invented to provide a progress measure that was disconnected from reality and had no impact on learning.

But it kept senior leaders, governors, and external agencies happy.

Cracks quickly emerged when primary schools realised that, unlike with levels where pupils could move further up the scale, now they were effectively constrained within the parameters of the year's curriculum and could only make 'expected progress'. This resulted in a proliferation of attainment categories: first, a 'mastery' or 'greater depth' band that acted as an end-of-year bonus point, then six-point systems to satisfy those schools that wished to track every half term, and even decimal systems where, for example, a Year 5 pupil could progress from 5.0 to 5.9 across the year. The systems many schools were using were in no way linked to what was happening in the classroom; they were simply a reflection of how many data drops a school had or how much progress they wanted to show. The more bandings you had in your system, the more progress you could apparently prove.

Meanwhile, secondary schools were focusing their attentions on creating new flightpaths to visualise and quantify pupil progress. In many schools, pupils were assigned 'working towards' grades based on a target derived from their on-entry assessment or previous Key Stage result. By assigning predicted GCSE grades on an ongoing basis and comparing to their targets, pupils could be described as working below, within or above their target band. By going further and assigning a value to the target descriptor – below = −1, on target = 0, above = +1 – schools could aggregate the data into a quasi-value-added score for the cohort, which could then be presented to governors, for example.

Other secondary schools employed a system of 'working at' grades, which commonly involved counting back a grade per year from a target grade to produce an expected grade for each year. These supposedly reflected the grade a pupil might achieve if they were to take the final exam at that point. In some cases, these annual 'working at' grades were subdivided to provide a termly increment – 7.1, 7.2, 7.3 and the like – to allow for supposedly finer measures of progress. Such approaches resemble those adopted by many primary schools.

There are several problems with the flightpath approaches outlined above: 1) they assume that progress is linear for the convenience of a measure; 2) they use GCSE grades outside of Key Stage 4 where no such grades exist; 3) they use GCSE grades to describe individual pieces of work, or to label pupils, which was one of the main issues with levels; 4) simplistic attempts to calculate value added will not match government measures such as progress 8, and therefore lack credibility; 5) such grades alone do not provide useful information about learning; 6) the grades are not derived from standardised assessment, they are effectively guesswork; 7) they give the illusion of consistency and comparability between cohorts and subjects.

Many of the approaches adopted by both primary and secondary schools for the purpose of measuring progress are hugely flawed, distracting, and – if they require significant data gathering – a potential workload issue. Schools need to question why they need these measures and what impact they have on pupils' learning. If, after investigation and discussion, it is decided that their impact in the classroom is positive and the efforts required to generate them are justified, then carry on. However, if the measures are abstract, devised purely to satisfy the data demands of governors and external audiences, and are recreating the issues of levels, then schools should consider changing tack.

Essentially, in-school measures of progress will almost certainly result in the reinvention of levels in some form or other; and usually these new levels will be based on teacher assessment, which is subjective and prone to distortion. The higher the stakes, the higher the risk. We cannot expect accuracy if we: a) convert a human opinion into a number; b) subtract one number from another to gauge progress; and c) use the results to judge school performance from the classroom upwards.

Progress is not a single, simple, definable thing. It is not distance, or time, or weight and there is no SI unit with which to measure it. Progress is a complex, multi-faceted, four-dimensional entity involving periods where new knowledge and skills are grasped, old concepts are revisited, gaps are filled, understanding is secured and deepened, and barriers to learning overcome. Sometimes progress does not involve covering more of the curriculum; 'sometimes progress is simply about consolidation' (Commission on Assessment without Levels, 2015: 12). And to further complicate matters, there are a host of other contextual factors that can help or hinder a child's development. With this in mind, schools would do to well ask themselves the question posed by Becky Allen (2018):

> *What if we cannot measure pupil progress?*

If the answer to this question is 'we can't' – which it most likely is – then this is hugely inconvenient for those schools whose systems are geared towards this end, for whom progress measures are the main reason for collecting data.

We will revisit the issue of progress measures again in Chapters 7 and 9 and will discuss more meaningful and effective approaches that schools can adopt.

2.5 Software systems

Schools use management information and tracking systems to store and analyse all manner of data: contextual information, bespoke groupings, results of statutory assessments, test scores, teacher assessments, targets, and information relating to pupils with SEND including provision mapping and the outcomes of diagnostic assessments. In theory, these systems save time by allowing teachers instant access to all this information, by analysing large amounts of data quickly, and compiling analyses into useful, easy-to-interpret reports. Such functionality is vital to the smooth running of a school.

Ideally, systems are highly customisable, thus allowing schools to store and analyse any data in any format for all subjects and pupils at any point the school chooses. In reality, however, this is often not the case, and it is then that systems can influence both the type and frequency of the data that schools collect.

The systems schools put in place to store, analyse and report their data should be the final part of the jigsaw. They should be implemented after the school's assessment policy and data strategy have been written, so that everyone is clear on how and when pupils will be assessed, what data will be produced and what that data will be used for. Then and only then should a school design or select a system, ensuring that it matches its current requirements and can be easily customised to adapt to future changes as the strategy develops. Installing a system before these decisions have been made will result in compromises and potentially risk the system dictating the format and timing of data and reports. There are too many senior leaders and teachers struggling on with systems that do not mesh with the school's ways of working, resulting in confusion, frustration, and increased workload for staff. The golden rule is: if the system isn't working, get a new system.

We will return to the issue of tracking systems in Chapter 7.

2.6   A licence for change

In order to dataproof themselves – to adopt practices that are more focused on teaching and learning, and less influenced by the pressures of accountability – schools need to break down the barriers to change and cut out the noise from those that seek to maintain the status quo. This is easier said than done when the stakes are high, and the noise is coming from the various departments and agencies of government. But now the tide has turned. In the years since the removal of levels in England, those same agencies that once drove schools to measure more, more often, have sought to support and encourage schools in their efforts to overhaul and improve their approaches to assessment and data collection. It is likely that the main factors behind a resistance to change are now local. Internal factors relating to software systems, performance management, target setting and reporting requirements, combined with external influences from local schools, authorities and consultants can all prevent a school from making necessary changes that will improve the quality and flow of information. Resistance to change may be due to inertia or it may be active and aggressive. Either way, the issues need to be challenged and overcome if a school is to take control of its data.

In an acknowledgement of the state of the situation, and perhaps in an attempt to force change, Ofsted has gone for the nuclear option of disregarding school data entirely during inspection. Whilst initially a shock to the system – and frustrating for those schools that have a high degree of confidence in the accuracy of their data – it does provide an opportunity. If schools were producing data for Ofsted, and Ofsted is no longer going to look at it, then why produce data? It has forced schools to question the nature and purpose of the data they collect, and finally given licence to those schools that have perhaps resisted or been prevented from making changes in the past.

This volte-face by Ofsted was not a sudden decision; it had been building since 2014 when the decision was taken to remove national curriculum levels. In 2015,

Ofsted released a short video, which aimed to explain the inspectorate's position on the use of data. In it, Sean Harford, Ofsted's National Director for Schools, explained that

> Inspectors will use lesson observations, pupils' work, discussions with teachers and pupils and school records to judge the effectiveness of assessment and whether it is having an impact on pupils' learning. They don't need to see vast amounts of data, spreadsheets, charts or graphs. Nor are they looking for any specific frequency or type or volume of marking or feedback. (DfE, 2015)

In September 2015, the same month the final report from the Commission on Assessment Levels was published, Ofsted brought out a new inspection framework, which, for the first time, contained 'myth-busting' statements that sought to clarify what inspectors did and did not expect to see during an inspection. On the subject of data, the guidance stated

> Ofsted does not expect performance- and pupil-tracking information to be presented in a particular format. Such information should be provided to inspectors in the format that the school would ordinarily use to monitor the progress of pupils in that school. (Ofsted, 2018a[2015]: 14)

This was a vital and empowering statement in that it gave schools the freedom to adopt meaningful approaches to assessment tracking, rather than collect data in a format designed solely for the purposes of proving progress to Ofsted.

In 2017, Ofsted went further, releasing an important update that tackled the thorny issue of 'expected progress'.

> 'Expected progress' was a DfE accountability measure until 2015. Inspectors must not use this term when referring to progress for 2016 or current pupils. (Ofsted, 2017: 7)

This was ground-breaking because up until that point many inspectors were still requiring schools to provide some form of data that quantified the progress each pupil had made across the year or key stage and gave the proportions making 'expected progress'. This expectation drove schools to maintain levels-style approaches to progress with all their inherent flaws. In many cases, schools simply continued using the system they had always used for the sake of convenience, despite knowing they were at odds with the modern curriculum. This short statement gave them a defence, not just against inspectors asking for inappropriate data, but against others, too. The gloves were off.

Then in June 2018, Amanda Spielman, Her Majesty's Chief Inspector, gave a speech at the Bryanston Education Summit, which strongly hinted at Ofsted's direction of travel. On data, she remarked

we do not expect to see 6 week tracking of pupil progress and vast elaborate spreadsheets. What I want school leaders to discuss with our inspectors is what they expect pupils to know by certain points in their life, and how they know they know it. And crucially, what the school does when it finds out they don't! These conversations are much more constructive than inventing byzantine number systems which, let's be honest, can often be meaningless. (Spielman, 2018)

Ofsted were moving even further away from their datacentric past towards a more conversation-based approach. The speech also questioned the 'merit in trying to look at every individual sub-group of pupils at the school level':

It is very important that we monitor the progress of under-performing pupil groups. But often this is best done at a national level, or possibly even a MAT or local authority level, where meaningful trends may be identifiable, rather than at school level where apparent differences are often likely to be statistical noise. (Spielman, 2018)

This was a significant step. Schools have always known that monitoring the progress of small groups of pupils and the gaps between them is a fool's errand, but they did it anyway because it was expected of them. But here was Ofsted finally admitting the folly, therefore allowing schools to reassess their reporting requirements, including the supply of data to governors and other external agencies. It is worth noting that until 2015, schools in England were subject to scrutiny based on the contents of a 100-page RAISE report, much of which related to the supposed performance of numerous pupil groups. This has since been replaced by a narrative-based and context-rich Inspection Data Summary Report (IDSR), which, in its current guise, is a mere six pages long, none of which is devoted to the performance of groups.

July 2018 saw the publication of another update from Ofsted, which clarified their use of the term 'tracking':

Use of the word 'tracking' in inspection reports is problematic as it can suggest that some form of numerical data is required, when there is no such requirement, even in English and mathematics. (Ofsted, 2018b: 9)

Ofsted had moved from a position of expecting internal data in a particular format, to telling schools they could use whatever data they liked, to suggesting that they didn't need any internal data at all.

Perhaps the most significant report published in recent years is *Making Data Work*, written by Professor Becky Allen (Teacher Workload Advisory Group, 2018). It has had a major influence on Ofsted, laying the ground for their move away from a reliance on internally generated data, and should be read by all involved in the field of school improvement, including local authorities, MATs and governors.

The report's key points include the following:

- School leaders should not assume that group analysis of attainment will be more informative than whole class analysis. The smaller the groups being compared, the more likely that any differences observed are simply statistical noise.
- Ofsted inspectors should ask questions about whether schools' attainment data collections are proportionate, represent an efficient use of school resources, and are sustainable for staff.
- Amend performance-management guidance to clarify that objectives and performance management discussions should not be based on teacher-generated data and predictions, or solely on the assessment data for a single group of pupils.
- Beyond statutory data collections (such as the results of Key Stage 1 assessment), do not request regular attainment data from schools unless they meet a trigger for intervention.

It also makes specific recommendations for governors:

- Governors should be prepared to receive information in whatever form it is currently being used in the school. They should agree with school leaders what data they need, and when, in order to fulfil their role effectively and to avoid making unreasonable, ad hoc data requests during the course of the school year.
- Governors should not routinely see teacher judgement tracking data and in-school testing data if it has no external reference, as it is of limited use to them.
- Governors should also consider whether data is proportionate, how school leaders are collecting it, and the frequency and time costs of data collection. They should understand the limitations of attainment, progress and target-setting data, and be able to access training on the effective use of data on pupil performance.

The inevitable culmination of this protracted process came in 2019 with the publication of Ofsted's revised *Education Inspection Framework*, which states that 'Inspectors will not look at non-statutory internal progress and attainment data on section 5 and section 8 inspections of schools' (Ofsted, 2021). This was a hugely significant step that finally gave schools a licence to change.

2.7　Summary

Schools can and must adapt assessment and data systems to ensure they are focused on supporting pupils by providing teachers with useful information, whilst also supplying proportionate amounts of data to relevant key audiences such as parents and governors. Schools need to understand the power of data but also its limitations, and should assess whether workload involved in the collection and processing of data is justified in terms of its impact on learning. They must also acknowledge the stresses that will lead to the distortion of data and seek to minimise those as much as possible. Addressing all these issues will allow a school to develop a coherent and sustainable data strategy.

And that is the aim of this book.

References

Allen, B. (2018) What if we cannot measure pupil progress? [Online]. Available at: https://rebeccaallen.co.uk/2018/05/23/what-if-we-cannot-measure-pupil-progress/ (Accessed 4 May 2021).

Christodoulou, D. (2016) *Making Good Progress?* Oxford: Oxford University Press.

Commission on Assessment without Levels (2015) *Commission on Assessment without Levels: Final Report* [Online]. Available at: https://assets.publishing.service.gov.uk /government/uploads/system/uploads/attachment_data/file/483058/Commission_on _Assessment_Without_Levels_-_report.pdf (Accessed 4 May 2021).

Department for Education (DfE) (2015) Sean Harford talks about what inspectors will look at when considering a school's assessment system [Online]. Available at: https://www. youtube.com/watch?v=H7whb8dOk5Q (Accessed 5 May 2021).

Department for Education (DfE) (2020) *Schools Causing Concern* [Online]. Available at: https://assets.publishing.service.gov.uk/government/uploads/system/uploads/attachment _data/file/922910/schools_causing_concern1.pdf (Accessed 5 May 2021).

Education Endowment Foundation (n.d.) *Assessing and Monitoring Pupil Progress* [Online]. Available at: https://educationendowmentfoundation.org.uk/tools/assessing-and-monitoring -pupil-progress/improving-teacher-assessment/ (Accessed 5 May 2021).

Ofsted (2017) School Inspection Update March 2017 [Online]. Available at: https://assets. publishing.service.gov.uk/government/uploads/system/uploads/attachment_data /file/595739/School_inspection_newsletter_March_2017.pdf (Accessed 5 May 2021).

Ofsted (2018a[2015]) *School Inspection Handbook* [Online] Available at: https://assets. publishing.service.gov.uk/government/uploads/system/uploads/attachment_data/ file/730127/School_inspection_handbook_section_5_270718.pdf (Accessed 19 May 2021).

Ofsted (2018b) School Inspection Update July 2018 [Online]. Available at: https://assets. publishing.service.gov.uk/government/uploads/system/uploads/attachment_data /file/723268/School_inspection_update_060718.pdf (Accessed 5 May 2021).

Ofsted (2021[2019]) *School Inspection Handbook* [Online]. Available at: https://www.gov.uk /government/publications/school-inspection-handbook-eif/school-inspection-handbook (Accessed 4 May 2021).

Spielman, A. (2018) Amanda Spielman at the Bryanston Education Summit [Online]. Available at: www.gov.uk/government/speeches/amanda-spielman-at-the-bryanston-education -summit (Accessed 5 May 2021).

Teacher Workload Advisory Group (2018) *Making Data Work: Report of the Teacher Workload Advisory Group* [Online]. Available at: https://assets.publishing.service.gov.uk /government/uploads/system/uploads/attachment_data/file/754349/Workload_Advisory _Group-report.pdf (Accessed 4 May 2021).

Treadaway, M. (2015) Why measuring pupil progress involves more than taking a straight line [Online]. Available at: https://ffteducationdatalab.org.uk/2015/03/why-measuring -pupil-progress-involves-more-than-taking-a-straight-line/ (Accessed 4 May 2021).

GENERATING AND COLLATING HIGH-QUALITY DATA

3.1 What information do you need and what do you want it for?

As we saw in Chapter 2, schools in England have a clear licence to change when it comes to pupil data. What's more, in an increasingly autonomous educational system, schools are expected to make decisions which actively benefit the pupils they teach, rather than to react to external diktat. The legacy of external demands and the defensive reaction of many schools to an accountability system which has often appeared to be mercurial at best has left many in education uncertain as to how to move forward. Rather than being dataproof, many schools have found themselves beholden to bad data, as we outlined in the previous chapter.

Whilst much of the questionable data within the school system has often been related to attainment and progress, this is not the only area that schools need to consider when considering which data to generate and collect. The focus on attainment data has often led to a neglect of other categories of data which provide valuable insight into the challenge facing schools.

To become a dataproof school, those responsible for school data need to ensure that the lessons of the past have been learned. Understanding the many ways in which data can be compromised is essential. Ensuring that all of those in the system understand both the limitations and the benefits of information that is generated in school is vital. We looked at the effects of external accountability pressures in Chapter 2; this chapter will consider what schools need to know about generating high-quality internal data.

Schools do not start without some degree of institutional knowledge and historical data, of course. But what if that was the case, and there was no prior knowledge within the system?

The answers to this question will help you to understand your own circumstances; and taking some time to consider this question will reap considerable benefits. If you lost your database, how long would it be before the lack of information would have an impact on what happens within your school? Which data would you collect in order to replace what you had lost?

This begs questions about what schools actually do with the data they gather. For now, imagine that you and all of the people who work in your organisation know nothing whatsoever about the pupils in your school, or how to go about collecting the information you would want to have. What should you want to know and how should you go about gathering that information?

As we noted in Chapter 1, teachers and school leaders need four main categories of data:

- Contextual information
- Attainment data
- Development
- Additional provision.

This chapter will provide an overview of the issues which need to be understood in order to generate and gather this information.

3.2   Contextual information

A great deal is now known about the impact of pupil-centred factors on children's development. Knowing the context of the pupils in a school is clearly important when it comes to understanding how to support individuals and cohorts of pupils.

Schools routinely collect and record information on children's month of birth, sex and ethnicity, as well as any identified special educational needs or disabilities, Free School Meal status and home languages. In addition, schools frequently use indices of deprivation to provide contextual information for the pupils they teach. Each of these categories has an impact on group outcomes, as shown by Leckie and Goldstein (2019: 521) amongst others, with, for example, older children recording higher attainment on average than their younger peers, and those living in more deprived postcode areas making less progress than their peers who live in less deprived areas.

Whilst group outcomes do not suggest anything about individual outcomes (the variation within each group is always greater than the variation between groups), recognising that certain groups face greater challenges is clearly important when planning teaching and learning provision.

When it comes to age, for example, younger pupils within a cohort generally have slightly greater challenges than their older peers. Whilst the group effect diminishes over time, there continues to be an impact throughout the period of statutory education (Sammons et al., 2014: 29). Schools routinely collect pupils' dates of birth, and it is therefore relatively simple to group pupils by month of birth. Grouping by term of birth – splitting cohorts into three four-month groups of autumn, spring and summer – can be useful when considering whether age may be an important factor for particular classes or cohorts within your school. The middle of the school year is 3rd March; constructing a statistic which indicates mean age in days either side of this date can provide teachers with useful information about their pupils.

Age data is accurate inasmuch as a child's date of birth is generally recorded accurately; recording any anomalies in the circumstances of birth may be useful as this can have an effect on a child's age relative to their peers. In a class of 30 children, for example, two will have been born prematurely (National Institute for Health and Care Excellence (NICE), 2015). These children are at greater risk of neurodevelopmental disability compared to their peers. Those born prematurely in July and August are often placed in cohorts one school year above the cohort they would have been with had they been born at term.

Pupil ethnicity may be important within a particular context, especially as this information is often, in our experience, subject to error. Ensuring that ethnicity is recorded accurately, with the right level of detail depending on your context, is vital if you decide to gather and collate this data. Inaccurate or outdated information can compromise inferences or decisions that are made in your school, and data should be regularly checked and updated.

When it comes to ethnicity, schools are often interested in the languages spoken at home by pupils. Depending on context, this may be important information which you gather. Once again, ensuring that this data is accurate and up to date is crucial. Additionally, you may wish to track changes over time as this may inform decisions which you make regarding support for your pupils.

Where special educational needs and disabilities have been identified by school, these will usually be recorded in some detail. As SEND changes over time for many pupils, your system should allow you to record these changes. Likewise, children who receive Free School Meals should be recorded, with detail of changes over time. In some cases, children who are eligible for Free School Meals do not take them up; where it is possible to record this information, you should consider doing so.

Information on pupil mobility should be collated as group outcomes for children who are educated in different schools are on average lower than those with high stability. The date pupils joined schools should be recorded. Pupils who join schools at the beginning of the autumn term are systematically different from those who join at the beginning of the spring and summer terms, and those pupils are systematically different from those who join at any other point in the school year. Once again, this data has no direct indication for any individual.

Pupils' medical and developmental experiences may have an impact, and you should consider how you might collate this information. This can be particularly important in Early Years education where children have had adverse experiences before statutory school age which might not be routinely recorded. As children move through education, recording significant medical and developmental experiences becomes easier and you should consider how you record this information.

As noted in Chapter 1, a further key principle for a dataproof school is that children should be in school, in class, focused and learning. Generating and recording information regarding the last of these is the focus of assessment systems, which we will consider below. In a dataproof school, attendance data is used to monitor whether children are in school; whilst most pupils attend regularly, those pupils who do not should be monitored and categorised so that appropriate support can be put in place.

In some contexts, some pupils are frequently out of class for a variety of reasons. Once again, this will not affect most pupils, but those who are affected should be monitored, categorised and supported.

A great number of schools gather and collate data on pupil focus; a majority of secondary schools have some way of tracking the perceived efforts of pupils, as do a small number of primary schools. Whilst there is clearly a cost to gathering and collating this information, as a dataproof school you should consider whether this is information on which you might act. If it is, it should become part of your contextual data.

Ensuring that contextual information is regularly updated and checked is vital, as is the recording of changes over time to ensure that each pupil, class and cohort within your school is given the support they need.

Box 3.1

Contextual data – a checklist

Date of birth
Month of birth
Term of birth
Circumstances of birth
Ethnicity
Languages in the home
Identified SEND
Free School Meal status
Previous schools
Date joined school
Medical experiences
Developmental experiences
Attendance
Time out of class
Pupil focus

3.3   Attainment data

A great deal of the information which teachers and those responsible for managing schools want to know concerns the academic attainment of the pupils in their charge. Schools wish to understand what has been learned over time, and which, if any, pupils have not advanced as much as their peers. Furthermore, teachers and school leaders want to benchmark their pupils against national standards. Teachers in England are expected to consider pupils' prior attainment when planning learning. Those responsible for holding school leadership teams to account are expected to use information regarding academic outcomes for pupils as part of their roles.

However, assessing pupils is not straightforward. Misconceptions about the purpose and accuracy of assessments are widespread, in our experience, and much of what is inferred as a result of assessments is not warranted. In some cases, it is actively inaccurate and leads to questionable actions, which further diminish the quality of the information about pupils.

Much has been learned about the complexities of assessing pupils, and a dataproof school should have a knowledgeable workforce which seeks to minimise the risks to data integrity. Understanding the inherent limitations of assessment data as well as the benefits of high-quality assessment information is key to becoming a dataproof school.

This section is necessarily comprehensive, and a dataproof school should ensure that those responsible for the generation, collation and analysis of data have had the opportunity to explore these issues fully. Regular revisiting of the issues here, ideally on an annual basis, should become part of your school's ongoing continual professional development.

Assessment of pupils is generally split into formative assessment – the inferences teachers make as they teach – and summative assessment – the summaries of what has been learned at any given time. Formative assessment is by its nature extremely subjective, as it relies on teachers attempting to make judgements as to what they believe pupils know and can do. Summative assessment is in most cases an attempt to be more objective, often utilising some form of standardisation to assist in the process.

In Chapter 2, we have already considered the distortions which might affect assessment data because too much weight is placed on the data. Much of this can be summarised by Goodhart's Law, often phrased as 'When a measure becomes a target, it ceases to be a good measure'.

It is important that those responsible for generating and utilising assessment data in a dataproof school understand what is known about the limitations of assessment data, and that they understand four essential concepts in assessment: Bias, Error, Reliability & Validity, and Utility.

3.3.1 Bias

There are two key types of bias to consider when assessing pupils: teacher bias and test bias. Teacher bias may be better thought of as 'human bias', because as Daisy Christodoulou (2015) says, 'Teacher assessment is biased not because it is carried out by teachers, but because it is carried out by humans'. Test bias refers to distortions which might undermine the inferences which might be made based on the results of a test.

When considering teacher bias, we need to look at the way in which teachers have been asked to generate assessment data for the pupils they teach. At the end of the Early Years Foundation Stage (EYFS), for example, teachers are asked to make judgements against 17 early learning goals (DfE, 2020: 27–31). At the end of Key Stage 1, teachers must make judgements against multiple criteria for reading, writing, mathematics and science (DfE, 2017a: 2). At the end of Key Stage 2, teachers must make judgements against multiple criteria for writing and science (DfE, 2017b: 2). Recent changes to GCSE assessments removed much of the requirement for teacher assessment, until the Covid-19 pandemic of 2020–21 forced Ofqual to ask schools to provide teacher-assessed grades in the absence of examinations.

Teacher assessment against standardised criteria is subject to bias, as numerous studies have shown (Bew, 2011: 49). One particular concern is that disadvantaged pupils are often under-assessed, as are children who have behaviour difficulties or special educational needs. Attempts to improve the reliability of teacher assessments often have huge time and effort costs as schools attempt to moderate judgements made by their teachers, and do little to reduce the bias identified by researchers.

Whilst it is almost impossible to teach in England without ongoing formative assessment, using biased human beliefs to make summative judgements is clearly hugely problematic. This age-old problem led to standardised summative tests being developed, in an attempt to reduce the human error in assessing individuals.

Tests also suffer from bias, unfortunately. As noted above, test bias refers to systematic distortions in test scores, which might undermine the inferences that might be made from the test. Tests have numerous limitations which we explore further in Chapter 4 when we look closely at using standardised tests. In summary, a test uses items which sample a domain of knowledge in order to allow inferences to be made about a pupil's position relative to their peers.

The most obvious elements which might introduce test bias for individuals are cultural and linguistic factors. Some students might get better scores because their cultural and linguistic knowledge benefits them when they take the test. Test bias can also arise from group factors, such as intense test preparation. Bias is further complicated because frequently there are genuine differences between groups who might take a test, and these differences arise not as a result of bias, but because of differences between groups. A simple example is the difference in mean test scores between those who have special educational needs and those who do not; whilst these means are often very different, this is not necessarily as a result of test bias.

Those who develop tests use a technique referred to as differential item functioning (DIF) to assess whether a test item shows any evidence of bias. This considers whether any particular item on a test is answered in a way which would not be expected given students' overall proficiency in the test. If items do suggest bias, tests can be reconfigured to reduce the bias where possible.

What should teachers and schools take from this? Teacher assessment is an essential element of teaching, but it is inherently inaccurate in ways which might disadvantage some pupils. Tests are generally unbiased and group differences often appear because there are, at group level, often genuine differences between groups. But even though tests are generally unbiased, in a dataproof school any test results which are unusual or unexpected when compared to teacher assessments are welcomed as an opportunity to investigate whether a pupil has been unconsciously under- or over-assessed.

3.3.2 Error

One concern which is frequently raised by teachers and school leaders is whether or not tests are accurate. This is often phrased as a negative, i.e. 'I think these test results are wrong, because…'. The reasons given vary, from a concern that a test does not accurately reflect the taught curriculum, to concerns that some questions are inaccessible to particular students for a variety of reasons. Whilst we will look closer at this issue in Chapter 4, it is worth considering the issue of error in assessment.

Once again, there are two aspects to consider: human error and test error. Human error is probably what comes to mind when you think about error – what if someone is simply wrong in their judgement? In assessment, error is different from bias, in that the error is inconsistent and may represent a positive or a negative inaccuracy whereas bias always works in one direction.

Human error in assessment can arise for many reasons, often related to time, effort and experience. It may, however, also arise from complexity, in that attempting to make absolute judgements about individuals is notoriously difficult. Humans tend to find comparative judgements – comparing two things and deciding which is better by some criteria – much easier, and we will look more closely at this in Chapter 5. In summary, human error can creep in easily when trying to make absolute judgements about individuals.

Test error arises because there is always a degree of uncertainty when measuring using a test. This uncertainty can be unnerving – many in schools would much prefer to be right than unsure – but it needs to be understood so that we can make the most of the assessments we have. This in turn will help to limit the human error when interpreting the results of assessments.

As you will recall from the discussion of bias above, a test uses items which sample a domain of knowledge (there is more about this in Chapter 4). Tests by definition consist of a limited number of items, or questions. Those who create tests identify two types of error which need to be considered: measurement error and sampling error.

Measurement error arises for a number of reasons. Any measurement tool which attempts to place results on a scale has a limited degree of accuracy, and when humans are involved in measurement, error can arise from a number of sources. With tests, an important source of error is pupils themselves. There are a great many things which can affect a pupil's ability to answer questions on a test (test anxiety, illness, energy levels, distractions amongst many others).

A second source of error in tests is inconsistency in scoring. This is a particular issue in the scoring of written work, or of portfolio work produced by students which we look at in Chapter 5. A further source of error comes from the choice of test items included in the test. Students may happen to know some things and not others, and the test may be inaccurate because of a particular student's unique experiences and knowledge.

Measurement error is most clearly different from bias when you consider how it manifests itself. Whereas bias always works in one direction either aiding or hindering a student throughout the test, measurement error can work in both positive and negative directions in individual test items. Scores cluster around a mean score which is called the 'true score', but some scores will have substantial positive or negative errors (perhaps because a pupil was in a negative state of mind during sections of the test as a result of a domestic issue, or their last-minute test preparation happened to include knowledge which featured in specific test items).

If a pupil were able to take the same test on multiple occasions, they would record a range of different scores due to measurement error. If a pupil took the same test one hundred times – which is clearly a theoretical proposition, for reasons which will be obvious – their scores would cluster around their true score. The range of scores can be modelled statistically, i.e. there are formulas which would allow you to create a range of scores around a mean score. This range is usually referred to as the margin of error.

Most tests that pupils take have limited numbers of test items, and whilst the measurement error can be minimised, it cannot be eliminated. This is one of the reasons qualification examinations are usually reported as grades rather than as numbers; a grade implies a degree of uncertainty whereas a score implies a degree of accuracy which is not justified.

Because measurement error is randomly distributed (i.e. it can be positive or negative and is more likely to be small rather than large) it can be reduced by aggregating several scores together as the errors cancel each other out. Several scores for the same child or scores of groups of children will reduce the effect of measurement error in most cases. Unfortunately, creating these groups, or samples of the wider population, introduces a different type of error.

Sampling error concerns the error introduced when scores are grouped together into samples of the wider population. Remember that error reflects the degree of uncertainty surrounding the results of a test. The smaller the group, the larger the sampling error. This is particularly problematic in small schools where very few children are assessed, but it may also arise in larger schools where a small number of pupils take a more esoteric examination. Where scores are 'disaggregated' – or split into even smaller groups – the issue is compounded.

As an aside, test scores have often been reported along with an indication of statistical significance. This is nearly always misleading, as Richard discussed extensively in *Databusting for Schools* (Selfridge, 2018: 183–5). Whilst a number that is deemed to be 'significant' may be worth investigating, it may also misdirect your effort and attention. In practice, test scores include some error but the more you understand what this means, the better you are able to use scores to make decisions which will benefit your pupils, teachers and schools.

What should teachers and schools take from this? Reducing human error is difficult and has cost implications. Measurement error is inherent in any test, and test scores may over- or under-assess those who take them. Sampling error should be considered when scores are aggregated together, and tests of statistical significance in school data are generally misleading.

3.3.3 Reliability and validity

When we assess children, we need to consider whether the assessments do what we want them to do. Given the potential effects of bias and error, are we certain that we have assessed children in a way that is as accurate and as fair as we can make it? And how certain can we be that it is reasonable to make the inferences we might want to make based on the assessments we have made?

As we have seen, relying on teacher assessment to create summative assessment is problematic, as a great deal of time and effort is required to ensure that assessments are consistent. What's more, however much effort we put in, we are still open to bias and error which are difficult, if not impossible, to eliminate.

When it comes to testing, these issues have been formalised in questions of 'reliability' and 'validity'. In what is now known as Classical Test Theory, the reliability of a test assumes that a test has a true score and an observed score (the true score plus an error score) and that it is possible to estimate the correlation between true scores and observed scores. Correlations range from 0 to 1, with 1 being a perfect correlation and 0 being no correlation.

Tests with perfect reliability are not ideal, as this tends to mean that the test is either not challenging enough or too challenging for those who take it. Getting all or none of the answers correct each time would both return a reliability of 1. A reliability coefficient of 0 means that test-takers get different questions right and wrong each time they take the test, which is equally undesirable.

Most tests are designed to have a reliability score of above 0.8, so anyone taking the test would get a very similar score if they took the test on a number of different occasions, answering similar questions correctly and incorrectly, with minimal bias or measurement error. This means, broadly, that reliability refers to the consistency of scores on a test rather than whether they are 'correct', as the word reliability might imply given its everyday use.

Validity is a property of the inferences that are made from the results of a test. Broadly, validity is the question of whether a test tests something meaningful which the test designers intended it to measure. Neither very easy nor very difficult tests have a great deal of validity as very little can be inferred from either test.

There are many other threats to the validity of a test, however. One of the greatest threats to the validity of a test is the placing of too much weight on its results. Where tests are used to judge the performance of those who teach the test-takers, for example, teachers and schools are actively incentivised to prioritise maximising test scores rather than learning. This can cause narrowing of curriculums, focus on test preparation and more – all of which will distort the test results and reduce the validity of the test.

Well-designed tests will have been through a process to assess their reliability and validity. The results can usually therefore be interpreted as having a reasonable degree of consistency and meaning, provided the administration of the assessment has been standardised and well administered. If the results have been standardised, they can provide even more information, as we discuss in Chapter 4.

Internally designed tests are unlikely to have been assessed for reliability and consistency. Any results should be understood in that light: they may tell you something about what a child can and cannot do, or what they do or do not recall, but they may also not be particularly consistent or meaningful. This is not to say that internal tests have no purpose, but it is to caution against making too many assumptions based on their results.

What should teachers and schools take from this? Well-designed tests are assessed to consider their reliability and validity. A test with a high level of reliability has a low margin of error. A well-designed test should test what the test designers plan that it should. Excessive preparation or test focus has a negative effect on the validity of a test. Understanding that tests can provide unbiased information against which to check teacher assessments is key to ensuring that test results are worth generating, collating and analysing.

3.3.4 Utility

Those who design and use assessments have become increasingly interested in what is referred to as the utility of assessment, or the utility of assessment methods. When proposed by Van der Vleuten, the utility of assessment methods was defined as the product of reliability, validity, educational impact, acceptability and cost (Van der Vleuten, 1996: 41). Whilst the concept of utility came from considerations within the medical education establishment – and therefore aspects of the idea relate to professional or certifiable examinations – the broad concept brings additional clarity to the issues facing the use of assessments.

Essentially, utility considers whether an assessment is worth doing. This is key in a dataproof school, as we want to ensure that schools generate, collate and analyse high-quality, useful data in order to make decisions about actions to support future teaching and learning.

Of the five aspects Van der Vleuten identifies, we have looked at reliability and validity above, leaving the educational impact, acceptability and cost of an assessment to be considered. Every assessment has a cost, in terms of time, effort and opportunity cost amongst others. These costs are a crucial consideration in schools. External assessments carry a financial implication. The burden of assessment often falls to teaching staff who have many calls on their time. The administrative demands of managing assessment data have wider implications for school-management teams. Time spent assessing takes away from other forms of teaching and learning.

Van der Vleuten's formulation includes the educational impact of assessment; however, as we know, assessment can have a positive effect on learning. The act of taking a test can help to embed knowledge through what psychologists call the Testing Effect. The content required for a test, the format of the test, the information gleaned through the administration of the test and the decisions about the programming of tests are all key factors when considering the educational impact of a test.

Finally, the acceptability of a test is a function of the views of pupils and their teachers about the test. Where teachers regard tests in a positive light, their response to preparing pupils or to administering and marking the test is different from the situation when tests are regarded negatively. Likewise, where pupils have positive views towards testing, their approach to tests is different from those who view tests negatively.

Whilst the concept of utility was developed in response to written tests, it has clear implications for teacher assessments too, as similar considerations can be used to evaluate the assessments made without utilising testing. Where assessments are deemed to be burdensome, costly, inefficient or educationally negative, they may have a negative effect beyond their simple administration.

An understanding of the issues surrounding the utility of assessment is crucial when it comes to understanding the limitations of assessment data. Unless those charged with generating assessment data understand the many potential negatives of the process, assessment data risks being compromised and may even have a negative effect on teaching and learning.

What should teachers and schools take from this? Consideration of the utility of a test helps to understand how to limit the potential threats to high-quality assessment and to high-quality assessment data. In a dataproof school, the costs of testing are taken into account, the educational impact of assessment is maximised and assessments are seen in a positive light by both those being assessed and those who use assessments as part of their ongoing monitoring of the development of their pupils.

Box 3.2 **High-quality assessment data – a checklist**

To develop high-quality assessment data, teachers and schools need to understand:

Bias

Error

Reliability and Validity

Utility

Given the limitations of assessment data, how should schools use the information which they generate? First, dataproof schools should expect their teaching staff to develop an in-depth knowledge of the pupils they teach. Whilst teacher assessment is by its nature impressionistic, teachers should be expected to be able to broadly categorise the pupils they teach into those who are working broadly at the expected level and those who are not. Where pupils are not working at the expected level, teachers should be able to group pupils into those working above and below the expected level for their age.

Second, standardised tests should be used to generate test scores, and these should be used as an unbiased check against teacher assessments for individual pupils. Using standardised scores, which we discuss in Chapter 4, schools should build up a picture over time as to where the school population fits when compared to the national population. Additionally, a picture should be developed of the educational development of individual classes and cohorts over time.

Ultimately, assessment should be used to identify those pupils who, for whatever reason, sit outside of the group of children who are making the development we expect of them at school and for whom additional provision is necessary, and those pupils who are broadly developing as we expect.

3.4   Development

As we noted in Chapter 1, the issue of development, or progress, over time has become somewhat contested, to the point that the word 'progress' has a number of separate and distinct meanings. Broadly speaking, these fall into two camps: 'numerical progress' (i.e. measures) and 'educational progress' (a more comprehensive review of the child's development and school improvement).

Since the Educational Reform Act of 1988, which introduced Key Stages to English education, English schools have been required to generate some form of number to summarise pupils' attainment at key points in their education. A similar system exists in the other parts of the United Kingdom in different forms, as well as in various countries around the world, as Richard discusses in *Databusting for Schools* (Selfridge, 2018: 214–18).

The numbers generated are used in a complicated system of calculating 'Value Added', which is held to be an indication of a school's performance. The outcome of this is an understanding that 'progress' is a number indicating how a pupil, a class or a school compares to others. As explored in Chapter 2, this has had a number of unintended consequences which have distorted what is meant by 'progress'.

In recent years, Ofsted has moved away from numerical progress and has redefined progress to mean 'knowing more, remembering more and being able to do more'. The two versions of progress are neatly summarised in the 2019 *School Inspection Handbook* (DfE, 2019: 223).

Evidence of impact should be drawn together from a combination of inspection activities. None of these on their own is sufficient to make an assessment of the impact. Inspectors will gather evidence of the impact of the quality of education offered by the school from the following sources:

- The progress that pupils are making in terms of knowing more, remembering more and being able to do more
- The nationally generated performance information about pupils' progress and attainment, where it is available in published national data.

This presents a challenge for dataproof schools, as use of the word progress is not always clear. We will attempt to reclaim the word in Chapter 9, but for now we will use the word development to describe the process of learning more as a pupil moves through school.

As we noted in the section on assessment above, we believe that assessment should be used to identify those pupils who sit outside of the group of children who are making the development we expect of them at school and those pupils who are broadly developing as we expect. This then allows a dataproof school to ensure that the data we generate, collate and analyse always leads to actions that support the teaching and learning in school.

As noted in Chapter 1, a further key principle for a dataproof school is that children should be in school, in class, focused and learning. Where data suggests that this applies for a particular pupil, a dataproof school will place this pupil in a category such as 'Making Expected Development' to indicate that there are no concerns about the pupil's development in school, and no additional provision has to be made.

Those children who have, for whatever reason, been assessed as being in advance of the majority of their peers should be placed in a category such as 'More Developed', and schools should decide how, or if, they wish to make additional provision for this group.

Most schools will then be able to identify their remaining pupils as 'Needing Support', as these pupils will need additional provision to help them to move into the 'Making Expected Development' or 'More Developed' groups where possible.

Some pupils may be categorised as 'Light Touch Monitoring' because they have needed additional support in previous years but are now in the 'Making Expected Development' group.

3.5   Additional provision

Much of the information about additional provision will be developed in conjunction with those responsible for Special Educational Needs and Disability (SEND). Summaries of this information should be brought into the school's main database to ensure that it can be integrated into the school's data strategy, which we will explore in Chapter 8.

3.6   Summary

In this chapter, we have considered what information you need and why you might want that data. We have focused on the benefits of high-quality data and the potential pitfalls which you face when you decide to gather information about pupils. A dataproof school will be aware of the potential misdirection which unwarranted assumptions might cause and how to avoid common data fallacies.

We have looked at the contextual data you should consider collating, the attainment data you should generate and how you might use that data to group children so that you can decide on the actions you might take to support individuals, groups, classes and cohorts where you deem it necessary.

In the next chapter, we will look at standardised testing and consider the information that you need to know to maximise their utility.

References

Bew, P. (2011) *Independent Review of Key Stage 2 Testing, Assessment and Accountability*. London: DfE.

Christodoulou, D. (2015) 'Why is teacher assessment biased?'. Available at: https://daisychristodoulou.com/2015/11/why-is-teacher-assessment-biased/ (Accessed 18 May 2021).

Department for Education (DfE) (2017a) *Teacher Assessment Frameworks at the End Of Key Stage 1*. London: DfE.

Department for Education (DfE) (2017b) *Teacher Assessment Frameworks at the End Of Key Stage 2*. London: DfE.

Department for Education (DfE) (2019) *School Inspection Handbook*. London: DfE.

Department for Education (DfE) (2020) *Early Years Foundation Stage Profile 2021 Handbook*. London: DfE.

Leckie, G. and Goldstein, H. (2019) 'The importance of adjusting for pupil background in school value-added models: A study of Progress 8 and school accountability in England', *British Educational Research Journal*, 45 (3): 518–37.

National Institute for Health and Care Excellence (NICE) (2015) *Preterm Labour and Birth*. London: NICE.

Sammons, P., Sylva, K., Melhuish, E., Siraj, I., Taggart, B., Toth, K. and Smees, R. (2014) *Influences on Students' GCSE Attainment and Progress at Age 16*. London: DfE.

Selfridge, R. (2018) *Databusting for Schools*. London: Sage Publications.

Van der Vleuten, C.P.M. (1996) 'The assessment of professional competence: Development, research and practical implications', *Advances in Health Sciences Education*, 1: 41–67.

STANDARDISED TESTS

4.1   Why use standardised tests?

Standardised tests can be an immensely useful part of a school's assessment system. Unlike teacher assessment, they provide unbiased information and can reveal gaps in learning that may not have been apparent; and unlike other types of tests, they provide vital external reference that shows how pupils in a school compare to others nationally.

Many tests, particularly those designed 'in house', simply provide a raw score and a percentage. This is adequate information if the interest is in those that meet or fall short of a threshold such as specified percentage, or – as is the case with a spelling or times tables test in identifying those that failed to answer all the questions correctly. A raw score or percentage will also allow the teacher to rank pupils in order and compare results to those of another class that have sat the same test. They could also track percentage of correct answers on consecutive tests over time to give an idea of improvement. But such data will not allow the teacher to find out how pupils' attainment compares to the national average. And this is where standardised tests come in – they provide that external, national reference. They do not tell us whether pupils have passed or failed. Instead, they place a pupil's result in context by showing where it ranks on the national bell curve. In so doing, they help us understand whether pupils are where we expect them to be based on, say, their prior attainment, and whether or not they are on track to meet targets. Internally designed tests are vital – and in many subjects they are the only option – but they cannot provide that national picture. It could be that an internal test is particularly hard, in which case the results will paint an overly pessimistic picture; or the test might be too easy, in which case the picture will be a flattering one. Standardised tests get round this problem by 'norm-referencing' – comparing all pupils to a representative national sample. Regardless of the difficulty of the test – although a well-designed test should be correctly pitched – pupils are compared against the sample average, and that will reveal their national position. Schools cannot easily obtain this national reference without standardised tests.

This chapter will look at standardised tests in detail. Topics covered include: sampling and norm-referencing; how standardised scores are calculated; the other types of data derived from tests; what tests are on offer and who provides them; the difference between fixed and adaptive assessment; test frequency; subjects covered; question- (or 'item'-) level analysis; and what the data does and does not tell us. The chapter is set out as a series of 'frequently asked questions', which we hope will provide an accessible and useful format.

4.2 What is a standardised test?

Unfortunately, there is no simple answer to this question. There are three main aspects to standardisation and a test need not conform to all of them to qualify as a standardised test. They are:

- Standardisation of items: all pupils take the same test with the same questions
- Standardisation of administration: all pupils sit the test under the same conditions
- Standardisation of scores: the raw scores are converted to a standardised scale to aid comparison of results over time and between subjects, to give an idea of where a pupil's attainment sits within the national population.

Most standardised tests used by schools do indeed meet all three criteria: they involve a fixed paper that all pupils in the year group take under the same conditions, the results of which are converted into standardised scores. It is, of course, possible for all pupils to take a test, the results from which remain as raw scores. Ostensibly, this may be considered a standardised test in that all pupils answered the same questions under the same conditions, but without the standardisation of scores we cannot infer a pupil's rank position in the population or compare results over time and between subjects.

Perhaps more confusing are those standardised tests that do not require all pupils to tackle the same questions, but which still generate standardised scores. Such tests – which are usually in multiple-choice format and taken on a computer – are known as 'adaptive' because each pupil's route depends on the answers they give: answer question 1 correctly, go to question 3; answer question 1 incorrectly, go to question 2. Pupils' paths through the test therefore bifurcate and a class's journey, if it were mapped out, would resemble a tree. Online adaptive tests, such as those offered by GL Assessment and Renaissance Learning, are becoming increasingly popular and will be dealt with later in this chapter.

In the main, however, the most popular form of standardised test is the fixed, paper-based, variety that are taken either annually or each term. Such tests usually focus on English (reading comprehension, grammar, punctuation and spelling), maths and science and are intended for a specific year group and, in the case of termly tests, point in the year. Cognitive ability tests (CATs) are also popular, particularly in secondary schools, where they are commonly used as a baseline assessment for the purposes of setting. Standardised tests for other subjects are not common and schools usually rely on school-generated assessments bolstered by within-department and inter-school moderation and comparative judgement. Online question banks are also being developed to cater for other subjects and these have the potential to generate standardised scores. More on that later.

In most cases, pupils will sit a common paper – or set of papers – alongside their peers. The resultant standardised score can be compared to scores from previous and future tests to monitor the pupil's position within the national population over time – information that is not provided by raw scores and percentages.

However, schools need to exercise caution when comparing individual scores and the average scores of cohorts and schools. First, standardised scores are noisy and differences between scores may not be as important as they seem. This is why some test providers place a margin of error – or a confidence interval – around each result: any difference between scores that is within the overlap of the confidence intervals is probably not telling us much. The other issue is the variable conditions under which the test is taken. If one school administers the test under strict exam conditions whilst another allows pupils to sit around tables in a normal classroom setting, then we probably should not compare the results of those two schools. Same goes for classes within schools. Standardisation of administration is vital if we want to compare results within and between schools. Even the day they take the test matters: one class takes the test on a sunny day; the other class takes it when it is blowing a gale. Can we compare the results with a high degree of confidence? Obviously, we can't control everything, but we should try.

4.3   What is a standardised score?

Unlike raw scores, standardised scores convey meaning by providing a common scale to aid comparison. In theory, a percentage of correct answers does this: it will allow results to be compared and ranked in order, and in some cases this is sufficient. But what can we learn from knowing that a pupil achieved 78% on a test? Was it an easy test or a hard test? How does this result compare to other pupils nationally? Can we compare percentages over time when the difficulty of tests may vary? Simple percentages have their limitations, and this is where standardised scores come in – they convey greater meaning.

For the purposes of this chapter, a standardised score is one derived from a standardised test and is in the range of <70 to >130 with an average of 100. The latter point is important: 100 equates to the average score; it is not the same as a scaled score of 100 that denotes the expected standard in Key Stage 2 tests in England. The difference between standardised scores and scaled scores will be covered later in this chapter.

The scores generated by most standardised tests are derived from a process known as norm-referencing and this relies on sampling:

A norm-referenced test is simply one on which performance is reported by comparison with a distribution of scores in some reference group. (Koretz, 2009)

First, the test provider selects a large sample to take the test – usually numbering thousands of pupils – which is stratified to ensure that it is representative of the wider population in terms of socio-economic characteristics, special educational needs, age and prior attainment. The initial results of the sample will be in the form of raw scores. The test provider can then calculate the mean score and standard deviation of the reference sample, which allows the calculation of the all-important z score of each possible result as follows:

$$Z = \frac{x - \mu}{\sigma}$$

where x = raw score, μ = mean score and σ = standard deviation.

A standard deviation gives an idea of the spread of results: a large standard deviation indicates a wide spread of results about the mean; a small standard deviation indicates a narrow spread of results. It is always the case that 68% of results are within one standard deviation of the mean score; 96% of results are within two standard deviations of the mean score. The z score shows how many standard deviations each possible result is from the mean score. It is important to note that z scores do not have to be integers; they can be fractions. In other words, a result could be 1.7 standard deviations above the mean or 2.1 standard deviations below it.

Once each result has been converted to a z score, it can then be converted to a standardised score using the following simple formula:

$$SS = Z \times 15 + 100$$

Regardless of the mean and standard deviation of the original raw scores of the sample, once converted to the standardised scale they will have a mean of 100 and a standard deviation of 15. This differs from usual presentation of a normal distribution with a mean of 0 and a standard deviation of 1. Adopting a mean of 100 and a standard deviation of 15 avoids negative scores. No one likes negative test scores.

These numbers are somewhat arbitrary. Any numbers could have been chosen, but the approach outlined above has become the standard method. On this standardised scale, therefore, 68% of results of the sample will be in the range 85 to 115 (100 +/– 15, i.e. within one standard deviation) and 96% of results will be in the range 70 to 130 (100 +/– 30, i.e. within two standard deviations). By converting the raw scores to standardised scores with an average of 100 and a standard deviation of 15, they now plot as a smooth bell curve and display a normal distribution (see Figure 4.1).

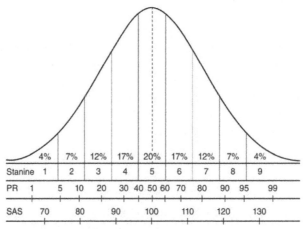

Figure 4.1.   Normal distribution showing stanines, percentile rank (PR), and standardised (age) scores (SAS). Note that pupils are not evenly distributed across the bell curve; there are more concentrated in the middle than there are at the ends.

Using the above formula to calculate the standardised score, we simple multiply the z score of each result by 15 and add 100. For example, a pupil sits a maths test and scores 62 out of 80. The sample against which they are compared has an average score of 50 out of 80 (which converts to 100) and a standard deviation of 10. We therefore know that our pupil's result is above national average and places them in the top 50% of pupils nationally. By subtracting the sample mean from the pupil's result and dividing by the sample standard deviation we obtain the pupil's z score:

$$(62 - 50) \div 10 = 1.2$$

The pupil's result is therefore 1.2 standard deviations above the mean, and their standardised score is calculated as follows:

$$1.2 \times 15 + 100 = 118$$

Fortunately, schools do not have to calculate the scores themselves. Test providers produce lookup tables that list the raw scores alongside the corresponding standardised scores or offer tools to calculate them. Online adaptive tests have the added advantage of automatic calculation without the need for additional data entry.

Standardised tests therefore provide schools with a score that tells them, with a fair degree of accuracy, where their pupils sit within the national population by comparing their results to those of a large sample that is representative of that population. This not only informs us about their level of attainment at the time they took the test, but also allows us to compare back to previous tests to check progress and compare to targets to check whether they are heading in the right direction.

It should be noted that standardised tests are reliable indicators of attainment for the majority of the population, i.e. those with scores between 70 to 130 – within two standard deviations of the population mean. They are less reliable when it comes to outliers – those pupils with the highest and lowest levels of attainment. The test may prove to be difficult to access for pupils with learning difficulties and may have few if any questions such pupils can answer. Very low results – scores below 70 – therefore tell us very little about a pupil's attainment. Likewise, due to the length of a test – it can't go on forever – it will naturally have a ceiling, and this means it may not provide us with a great deal of useful information about the 'most able'. In both cases, question level analysis will be a somewhat futile exercise. This will be dealt with further in Chapter 6.

4.4   Can schools standardise their own tests?

A school could, of course, devise their own test and norm-reference the results, but it is unlikely these will be as reliable as those from a true standardised test due to numbers involved and the demographics of the cohort. Is the school's population representative of the national population as a whole or is it significantly different? This is important because unrepresentative sampling will underestimate a pupil's performance or exaggerate it. In other words, comparing an average pupil to a low-performing cohort could make it look as if their attainment is well above average. Conversely, comparing an average pupil to a higher performing cohort could suggest they are performing significantly below average. Unless a pass mark is the main focus, internally generated standardised scores are more insightful than raw scores and percentages because they indicate a pupil's position in the cohort, but they lack the external reference of a nationally standardised test.

A group of schools, such a Multi-Academy Trust or local authority cluster, is in a stronger position in that it has a much larger group of pupils, which is more likely to be representative of the national population. This cannot, however, be assumed. Test providers employ rigorous procedures when sampling to ensure the norm-referencing is as reliable as possible. Groups of schools cannot randomly select pupils from a national population; they can only work with the pupils they have in their schools.

For English and maths, commercially available tests are the best option. However, due to the lack of tests in other subjects, running 'in-house' tests across multiple schools and standardising the results of the larger, more statistically viable pupil population is worth exploring.

4.5 What other types of data do standardised tests produce?

We have already discussed standardised scores, but there are other forms of data that we can gain from standardised tests.

4.5.1 Question level analysis

First, and perhaps most obvious, is the question- or item- level analysis: what the pupils got right or wrong. Teachers can get a good idea of a pupil's strengths and weaknesses just by marking a test, but some more formal analysis may be warranted. By entering answers into a spreadsheet, perhaps one used across a department, patterns may emerge and common gaps be revealed. Some companies provide their own software to do this, which can provide additional insight, i.e. it can show how a school's answers compare to those of other schools that took the test, or to the answers of the sample. Question level analysis can be carried out at several levels:

- Subject: percentage of correctly answered questions compared to national average
- Domain: as above but at subject domain level
- Pupil: percentage of questions each pupil answered correctly with breakdown of answers for each question
- Question: percentage of pupils that answered each question correctly.

However, unless the test is online or the test provider offers a marking service, any question level analysis will inevitably involve teachers entering a huge number of 1s and 0s onto a spreadsheet or online system. Schools must weigh up the benefits of such a process against the workload involved. Is the information gained from marking the test papers sufficient to support pupils' learning or is further analysis warranted?

4.5.2 Age standardised scores

Age standardised scores look the same as standardised scores, with a range of <70 to >130 and average of 100, but they have one key difference: they are adjusted to take account of age (NFER, n.d.a).

The process of calculating age standardised scores is almost identical to that of calculating standardised scores outlined above but with one extra step: before norm-referencing is carried out, the cohort is split into groups defined by month of birth. Therefore, rather than standardising the scores of the sample as a whole, the scores of each month of birth group are standardised separately and will therefore have their own separate bell curve. Whilst the ranges for each group will appear the same – <70 to >130 with an average of 100 – the raw scores that underlie the age standardised scores will vary. The average raw score of the September-born child is most likely higher than that of the January-born child, which in turn is higher than that of the August-born child, but all of those average scores convert to a value of 100 and will therefore be on a par with one another. Here we are dealing with what is and is not typical for a pupil born at a specific time of year, rather than what is typical for a pupil in the year group as a whole.

There is, therefore, a correlation – certainly for younger, primary age children – between standardised scores and pupils' month of birth: younger, summer-born pupils have lower scores; older, autumn-born pupils have higher scores. The 'normal', non-age standardised scores discussed in Section 4.3 could therefore mask other issues. For example, a September-born pupil may have above average scores that are low in comparison to similarly aged pupils; or an August-born pupil has below average scores that are relatively high in comparison to similarly aged pupils. Standardised scores might suggest that the autumn-born pupil is fine and that we should concentrate on the summer-born child when, in fact, the opposite might be true. More likely, we should focus on both cases but perhaps view them differently: the autumn-born pupil may have a learning difficulty, whereas the summer-born pupil shows attainment that is above average for their age but still needs to catch up.

Age standardised scores therefore make sense because they reveal issues that are not just a factor of a pupil's age. There is, however, one big issue with them: national tests and exams are not age standardised. Age standardised scores used to track towards future targets can therefore be misleading in that they can give the impression that summer-born pupils are doing fine, but only in comparison with other summer-born pupils. They can therefore paint a flattering picture that does not come to fruition in a national test.

In summary, age standardised scores are useful in that they help reveal issues that are masked by a pupil's age, but they are not necessarily so effective when monitoring progress towards non-age standardised targets such as exam grades. A simple solution is to use 'normal' standardised scores and group results by term of birth, and we will return to this in Chapter 9.

4.5.3 Confidence intervals

In some cases, a confidence interval will be provided alongside the standardised or age standardised score. This gives us an idea of the uncertainty – or 'noise' – around each result, which is extremely useful as it stops us from treating a pupil's score as a definitive, precise quantity. The result obtained on the test is known as the observed score. The true score, however, is not known and is likely to sit somewhere within the range of the provided confidence interval. If the level of confidence of the interval is stated as 90%, this implies that the true score of a pupil achieving that particular result – observed score – will lie within the range on 90% of occasions. In other words, if we tested that pupil again and again using tests of comparable difficulty, nine times out of ten their result will be somewhere within the range of the stated confidence interval.

Confidence intervals are especially useful when attempting to interpret changes in attainment over time. If the confidence intervals of scores on consecutive tests overlap, then we are looking at change that is within the margin of error. We should probably be more interested in cases where consecutive confidence intervals do not overlap; here the change is perhaps more unusual and therefore notable. That is not to say that former cases are not of interest. For example, there will be pupils that teachers will have hoped would show an increase in test scores after a gap in learning. In such cases, no change is perhaps a cause for concern.

4.5.4 Age equivalent scores

Many tests provide reading, spelling and even numeracy ages, which are particularly useful when reporting assessment data to parents due to their familiar, easy to understand format. Often referred to as age equivalent scores, these are an alternative way of presenting norm-referenced data whereby raw scores are converted into years and months rather than standardised scores. Comparing a pupil's age equivalent score to their chronological age gives an idea of how far above or below 'typical' they are, and – in theory at least – we could use age data to measure progress by looking at how the change in age equivalent score compares to the change in chronological age over a period of time. Perhaps a pupil's reading age has improved by 18 months over the school year. However, as with all measures, extreme caution must be exercised here. An age assessment is not an exact measure and comparing ages from successive tests will only compound the error. As a rule of thumb, a margin of error of six months should be applied to age equivalent scores – a reading age that is within six months of a pupil's chronological age is considered to be broadly typical – and this must be factored in when using such data to monitor pupil progress.

Age equivalent scores are certainly not pinpoint accurate. However, for schools struggling to find appropriate data to monitor the progress of the lowest attaining pupils, such as those with special educational needs, an age assessment is an attractive option as it can provide more meaning than standardised scores that are continually below 70. Often, a general standardised test will be inappropriate for use with such pupils, and more suitable, specific diagnostic tests should be sought.

4.5.5 Percentile rank

Percentile rank is a familiar and easy to understand measure. It simply tells us the percentage of pupils that achieved scores below the score in question. For example, if a pupil achieves a score that equates to the 75th percentile, it means it is higher than the scores of 75% of the sample. Their result therefore places them in the top quartile of pupils. A score of 100 – the average – is always at the 50th percentile (see Figure 4.1).

It is important to note that standardised scores are not evenly distributed across the percentiles due to the relatively small numbers of pupils achieving extremely high and low results. This means that there is a range of standardised scores associated with a single percentile at the top and bottom of the bell curve, whereas within the middle of the bell curve, where the majority are concentrated, the opposite is true. Scores of 133 upwards and 67 downwards are within the top and bottom percentiles, respectively. Meanwhile, in the middle of the curve, the range 99 to 101 – just three distinct scores – is spread across seven percentiles, from the 47th to the 53rd. For this reason, we must be very cautious inferring progress from a change in score. A change in score from 70 to 71 represents a shift from the 2nd to the 3rd percentile, whereas a change from 100 to 101 represents a shift from the 50th to the 53rd. Seemingly equal changes are therefore not always equal when it comes to percentile rank. They do, however, provide a useful tracking tool for schools not using standardised tests, especially secondary schools with large numbers. Tracking pupils' percentile rank in a cohort over time from entry is an effective way of illustrating their relative trajectories.

4.5.6 Stanines

Stanines – meaning 'standard nine' – are a different type of standardised score with a mean of 5 and a standard deviation of 2 and, as the name suggests, there are nine scores in total. Stanines are therefore much broader than common standardised scores, but this does not mean they are not useful. Sometimes we just want to group results together into broad bands and stanines provide a useful method for doing this.

You could, for example, use a simple progress matrix – a 9 × 9 grid – to compare a cohort's results from one term or year to the next. Here, standardised scores would be too granular – we don't want or need that much detail. Instead, we could investigate whether pupils have stayed in the same stanine between assessment points or moved up or down. Pupils moving up or down one or more stanines from one test to the next probably tells us more than a simple change in standardised score.

In a normal distribution such as the large, stratified sample used by test providers for norm referencing, 20% of results will be in stanine 5 (the middle band), 17% will be in stanines 4 and 6, 12% in stanines 3 and 7, 7% in stanines 2 and 8, and 4% in stanines 1 and 9 (see Figure 4.1). We could apply descriptors to these – average, well below, etc. – to provide more meaning, and test providers may suggest descriptors for stanines – or ranges of scores – in their guidance.

4.5.7 Scaled scores

Some test providers – Rising Stars and Renaissance for example – calculate scaled scores in addition to the standardised score. Here, rather than expecting the pupil to remain at broadly the same score from one test to the next, you will see them move along a scale, with expected scores for each assessment point and an expected rate of progress between them. Scaled scores of this type are intended to measure progress from term to term and year to year, and categorise that progress as below, within or above expectations. However, as with other types of data, scaled scores and associated rates of progress should be treated with caution. Pupils from different start points and with different needs will progress at different rates: progression may be roughly linear for some, whilst for others a period of rapid improvement may be followed by a plateau while they wrestle with new content. We must be cautious not to rely on data that suggests that all pupils progress at the same rate, just for the sake of convenience. We must also be aware of the 'noisiness' of test scores – a single score is not a definitive measure of attainment; a pupil's true score is never really known and will lie within a range around their observed score.

Note that in England, the term 'scaled scores' usually refers to results from national tests at Key Stages 1 and 2 (Department for Education, 2019). These are different from the proprietary scales described above and will be dealt with further in section 4.7.

4.6 Can standardised tests be used to measure progress?

Schools use standardised tests for a variety of reasons: to moderate teacher assessment, benchmark against national standards, predict future results, and for question level analysis. But perhaps one of the most frequently cited reasons is to measure pupil progress.

As discussed in Chapter 2, schools are often fixated on measuring progress, which is understandable when the national accountability system is built around such measures. It is therefore tempting to try to use standardised tests to second guess national measures. Unfortunately, it won't work and schools risk doing bad things with data in their attempts to do so.

When we have consecutive test scores it is perhaps natural to subtract the earlier one from the later one and treat the result as a progress measure. Sadly, this is too simplistic: the noisiness of test scores means they are just not that accurate. At best – if there are confidence intervals around the test scores – we could say that progress is 'in line with expectations' in cases where pupils' consecutive intervals overlap, and below or above expectations where they do not (National Foundation for Educational Research (NFER), n.d.b). We can then have three broad categories of progress and could monitor percentages of pupils in each over time. This is probably the best we can do but it does not – and cannot – match the value-added-style progress measures used in school performance tables.

The other issue is test content. We cannot compare the results of two tests and claim the difference to be a measure of progress if the two tests differ in their focus. Commercial tests should build from one test to the next, but that's not necessarily the case and certainly isn't if a school swaps test provider. Comparing test scores always comes with caveats; comparing the results of tests from different sources is extremely problematic.

If a school wants a simple measure of a cohort's progress, to present to governors for example, they could calculate the cohort's average percentile rank over time. This will indicate whether attainment is improving or not relative to other pupils nationally, and percentile rank is an easy concept to understand for most audiences. Change in average percentile rank, which could be negative or positive, can be viewed as a form of value-added measure. As always, the issue of noise applies (Allen, 2018) and we are unlikely to have a cohort-level confidence interval to help make sense of it.

4.7   What is the difference between standardised scores and scaled scores?

In theory, the terms are synonymous and interchangeable. Both involve the conversion of raw test scores into a common scale to enable comparisons of results on different tests: 32 out of 50 on one test might be on a par with 61 out of 80 on another once they have been converted to a common scale. In the English education system, however, they have distinct meanings (Tidd, 2018; Twist, 2018). The term 'standardised score' invariably refers to norm-referenced scores – those in the range <70 to >130 with an average of 100 – that are derived from commercially available tests. The term 'scaled score', on the other hand, almost always refers to those achieved in national tests at Key Stages 1 and 2.

If the scores were identical in every way except name, this would not be a problem. If the scores were markedly different in format and had distinct meanings, this would also not be a problem. Unfortunately, despite scaled scores from national assessments looking remarkably similar to those derived from other types of standardised tests – Key Stage 1 scores range from 85 to 115; Key Stage 2 scores range from 80 to 120; both have an 'expected standard' score of 100 – they are in fact very different. This similarity causes a great deal of confusion and it is vital that teachers understand the difference.

First, let us deal with the contrasting meanings of a score of 100. With standardised tests we are usually dealing with norm-referenced scores. Pupils' results are compared to those of a large, representative sample and their standardised score represents their relative position within that sample. This tells us approximately where their attainment lies within the national population. In such tests, a score of 100 is average: 50% of pupils achieve a score equal to or above 100 and 50% achieve a score below 100. The score of 100 is therefore the apex of the bell curve – the centre line – and any pupil achieving that score is regarded as average. In standardised tests it is not possible for more than half of pupils nationally to achieve a score of 100 or more and that is important, because in key stage tests in England, it is.

The difference between these two types of tests is the referencing. As already explained, standardised tests, such as those from commercial providers, are norm-referenced. Key stage tests in England, on the other hand, are essentially criterion referenced and here the score of 100 has been chosen to represent an expected standard rather than the average. As the name suggests, the threshold is linked to criteria: any pupil that meets the criteria achieves the expected standard and will receive a score of 100 or more. It is therefore possible for more than half of pupils nationally to achieve a score of 100 or more, and indeed in the tests taken at Key Stage 2 – at the end of primary education in England – around three-quarters of pupils do so in reading and mathematics. There are therefore far more pupils with scores above 100 than below, and the curve, unlike the normal distribution of most standardised tests, is skewed.

We must therefore be careful comparing standardised scores with the results of key stage tests which are seemingly equivalent but are the product of a very different process. The best way to compare these two sets of data is to convert them both into a common currency such as percentile rank. For primary schools in England, a standardised score of 94 could be adopted as a fairly safe proxy for 'expected standards' as it represents the attainment of the top two-thirds of pupils nationally. Whatever you decide to do, just be aware that scaled and standardised scores are not directly comparable.

4.8 Can standardised tests provide a suitable baseline assessment and predict future results?

The result of a test is just a snapshot of the child's ability, but it can provide a useful baseline because all pupils take the same test under the same conditions and the result does not depend on prior knowledge of the child. Standardised tests can also 'be highly predictive of performance in national tests and some may provide predictions as well as actual scores' (Education Endowment Foundation, n.d.).

Rising Stars and NFER tests provide an indication of whether pupils are working towards, at, or above expectations, which can help in predicting results. Others, such as GL Assessment's cognitive ability tests (CATs), provide estimates of results in future national assessments, which is a useful feature. These estimates, which represent the average final result of pupils with similar CAT scores, can be used as a target to track towards: is the pupil on target at interim assessment points? The estimate can also be used as a benchmark for a value-added measure. Once the pupil has taken their final exams, does their result exceed or fall short of the original estimate derived from the baseline test, and by how much? A cohort's value added can be calculated as the average difference between their actual and estimated results. Again, however, this is unlikely to match government measures.

Using a scatter graph, schools can also plot the results of standardised tests against final results to get an idea of likely outcomes for subsequent cohorts. A threshold in one test above which, say, 80% went on to pass a later test could be used as an indicator of the likelihood of current pupils achieving the same result.

This is where scatter plots are indispensable, and we will be dealing with those in Chapter 7.

4.9   Are standardised tests suitable for young children?

Using a standardised test as a baseline for progress measures is perhaps most controversial when it applies to the youngest children. An attempt to establish a baseline for pupils at the start of the reception year in primary schools in England – for pupils aged four – was first attempted in 2015. This involved a multi-provider approach and schools could choose the baseline they thought was most appropriate and effective. The baselines on offer varied widely from interactive iPad apps to table-top tasks carried out in a one-to-one scenario with a teacher, to 'non-intrusive' approaches where teachers observed children in the classroom environment and assessed against a checklist of criteria. The latter approach became the overwhelming favourite with teachers who wanted to avoid any unnecessary disruption in the early days and weeks of school.

Following a comparability study carried out by the Scottish Qualification Authority (SQA), which concluded that the results of the various baseline assessments were, unsurprisingly, incomparable (Standards and Testing Agency, 2016), the Department for Education decided to scrap the project and start again. This time there would be a stricter specification on the design of the baseline, and a one-to-one, task-based approach designed by NFER was decided upon (NFER, 2018). Whilst this is not a standardised test in the traditional sense of pupils tackling a test paper, or sitting at a computer answering multiple-choice questions, it is still standardised in that there is tight control over the tasks that the child attempts and the questions they answer. To maintain standardisation, the assessment is scripted – questions are read out word for word – and the teacher must set up the tasks in a specified way. It is also routed whereby the tasks attempted and the length of the assessment are dependent on the child's answers and how well they cope.

The controversy with this assessment is twofold. First, because it is a one-to-one assessment, it takes teachers' time away from the classroom during the first weeks of school when children are settling into their new environment. Second, it is designed to provide a baseline for a progress measure, the purpose of which is to hold schools to account when those children reach the age of eleven and leave primary education. The assessment is therefore not designed to provide teachers with useful, actionable information about children's early development. Indeed, the intention is to withhold the results of the assessment from schools to stop the score in any way influencing the child's education. The result is that schools will continue to make their own 'formative' baseline assessments in parallel to the statutory assessment so that teachers have the information they need in those early days of schooling.

Most schools making baseline assessments of the youngest children will take an in-class, over time, observational approach rather than a one-to-one, point-in-time assessment. But that does not mean that there is no merit in the latter, especially when carried out for screening and diagnostic purposes where standardisation is likely to be more accurate. Many test providers offer baseline assessments – some are the legacy of that initial attempt to establish a national baseline – and these are worth exploring if you want standardised data on young children. Such assessments usually provide results in the form of age-standardised scores, which are adjusted to take account of month of birth, a critical factor when assessing young children. These will help highlight differences in learning and development as opposed to those that are simply a factor of age.

Standardised assessments are available for the youngest children and can be powerful tools in the early diagnosis of learning difficulties. As with other forms of assessment, the problems start when the data is used to hold schools to account. This confuses the purpose of assessment, places it in tension, and can result in its distortion, ultimately rendering it unreliable.

4.10   What should I consider when choosing a standardised test?

Before choosing standardised tests for your school, you need to consider input and output – in other words, the target group (Who will take the test?) and the information (What do you want the results to tell you?). Is the test appropriate for and accessible to the children in your school, and will the data tell you anything you didn't already know about their learning? In Chapter 3 we discussed test validity (Is the test testing the right things?) and reliability (If the pupils took similar tests repeatedly, would the results be consistent?). These are crucial properties of the tests that need to be considered.

How big is the sample that the norm-referencing is based on? Is it a random, stratified sample, or simply a self-selecting sample of schools that have chosen to use that test? How regularly does the test provider re-standardise the test with a new sample? If this is done infrequently you may be comparing your pupils to a sample that took the test many years ago, which could give a false – and inflated – picture of standards.

Accessibility is another important factor. Consider very carefully whether it is appropriate to use tests intended for younger year groups to assess pupils with SEND, for example a Year 2 test for a pupil in Year 6. It may be useful if they are truly following the Year 2 curriculum, but for most this will not be the case and all the result will tell you is how that Year 6 pupil with SEND compares to Year 2 pupils in general. The question-level analysis may provide some insight, but the scores will not. Instead, consider using more appropriate tests that are specifically aimed at assessing the strengths and weaknesses of pupils with SEND and are therefore more accessible to such pupils. We will return to this in Chapter 6, where we will deal with assessment of outliers.

Schools will probably be most focused on the content of the test when selecting the best product to use, so key questions will focus on what the test is testing, whether it links to a new or out-of-date curriculum, and whether it has the right proportions of questions from each domain or focuses more heavily on certain areas. These are certainly valid considerations, but their relevance varies in importance depending on the purpose of the test. If your main aim is to use the test for formative purposes – to find out whether pupils have learnt what they have been taught – then curriculum alignment is vital. However, if your primary purpose is to find out how the pupils in your school compare to other pupils nationally, then these considerations are less relevant. The test is carefully designed to ask a range of questions that pupils of a particular age may or may not know in order to rank them in order. The test will therefore contain questions that most pupils will get right as well some questions that very few will be able to answer. Using tests for both formative and summative purposes requires a balance that is difficult to strike.

Another important factor is the format of the test. Do you want to use fixed, paper-based tests or could you perhaps use online, adaptive tests? The former are similar to the final tests and exams that pupils take as part of national, statutory assessment and are therefore better for test practice. They also ensure that all pupils attempt the same questions, which is often an important factor. The latter are quicker to administer and provide instant feedback but require adequate IT resources; and the questions – in multiple-choice format – do not resemble those of statutory assessments and will vary from pupil to pupil. Then there is the frequency of the test. Some are annual, and that may be sufficient if the purpose is to check on standards and monitor progress year on year. Other tests are administered each term, which may fit well with a school's assessment calendar as well as being better suited to a teacher's needs by revealing issues early on; and online, adaptive tests can be used even more frequently for regular checks of understanding. The frequency and format of the tests are therefore critical considerations when selecting standardised tests for your school.

4.11 What is an adaptive test?

Most standardised tests involve all pupils sitting the same paper and attempting to answer the same set of the questions. Adaptive tests are different because the route pupils take is governed by the answers they give: each subsequent question depends on the answer they gave to the previous one. Adaptive assessment is a complex process and requires tight control on possible answers in order to eliminate ambiguity, which is why they are generally computer based and involve multiple-choice questions. An example of a non-computer-based adaptive assessment is the NFER baseline assessment due to be administered to pupils at the beginning of the reception year in primary schools in England (NFER, 2018). Here, a teacher will set tasks for the pupil to attempt, but such approaches are labour intensive and are not a particularly efficient way of regularly assessing large groups of older children. For the purposes of this book therefore, adaptive assessment refers to the computer-based packages that many schools buy into. Popular examples include GL Assessment's New Group Reading Test (NGRT) and Star Assessments from Renaissance Learning.

Pupils that undergo an adaptive assessment will have an individual experience with different questions. Calculating a standardised score is therefore not a simple case of comparing a pupil's total score to a reference sample. Generating a standardised score from an adaptive test is more complicated and requires comparison at the question level. This means that two pupils who achieve the same raw score – and therefore the same standardised score – on a fixed test could achieve different standardised scores on adaptive tests if their strengths lie in different areas.

There are, of course, pros and cons to any form of assessment. Adaptive tests are quicker to administer and analyse, more personalised, fairer, and more effective at revealing pupils' strengths and weaknesses (Centre for Evaluation and Monitoring, 2020). However, they are mostly limited to multiple-choice question format, which does not reveal the steps taken to solve a problem, and they do not emulate national tests, making them less suited to preparation. Also, many schools may struggle to administer adaptive assessments if they lack sufficient IT resources.

4.12　What are the downsides to standardised tests?

A test is a snapshot and is not necessarily a fair assessment of a pupil's ability. Everyone has a bad day, and some will struggle with tests. Conversely, a student might get lucky and guess some answers correctly. Another issue is cramming for tests: the student can answer the questions on the day, but could they do as well if they were to take a similar test a month later? In addition, the test can never assess the whole domain, only a sample of it – it can never test everything a child knows. The law of diminishing returns applies here: you can seek to improve the reliability of a test by increasing its length in order to test more of the domain, but there is a limit to what is feasible, and children will lose interest and give up after a certain amount of time. This amount of time depends on age: perhaps a maximum of 20 minutes for the youngest children and 3 hours for an undergraduate.

There may also be a perception that the test will not tell the teacher anything they did not already know. This may be true some of the time but is unlikely to be the case for all classes and subjects all of the time. Even where no new information is revealed, having your judgement backed up by a standardised test – a second opinion if you like – is not such a bad thing. And where the test result contradicts the teacher's judgement, that should obviously raise questions about possible bias and pupils' performance on tests versus their performance in class.

No teacher should have to waste time running assessments for the sake of it. The primary purpose of a standardised test is to provide useful, actionable information for the teacher. If this is not the case, then consider using different tests or whether you need them at all. They should not be viewed as the arbiter of truth and the final word that overrules the teacher's judgement; rather they should be part of a wider assessment framework that is geared towards supporting children's learning.

4.13 Summary

Standardised tests are powerful tools and should be part of any school's wider assessment framework. They provide national reference, reveal gaps in learning, can help to monitor progress and even predict results. However, to be used properly they need to be understood, and that requires knowledge of their limitations and the common misconceptions that surround them. Standardised scores, for example, are not pinpoint accurate and comparing scores on consecutive tests is not a measure of progress. Moreover, norm-referenced standardised scores are not the same as the scaled scores derived from national tests conducted in primary schools in England, despite their apparent similarities. Perhaps most importantly, there is no one-size-fits-all approach: what works for the majority may not be appropriate for certain groups of pupils and other forms of assessment should be sought. Once these facts are understood and appreciated, standardised assessment in its various guises can tell you a huge amount about the learning of pupils in your school.

References

Allen, B. (2018) What if we cannot measure pupil progress? [Online]. Available at: https://rebeccaallen.co.uk/2018/05/23/what-if-we-cannot-measure-pupil-progress/ (Accessed 4 May 2021).

Centre for Evaluation and Monitoring (2020) 5 reasons to use adaptive tests [Online]. Available at: https://www.cem.org/blog/5-reasons-to-use-adaptive-tests/ (accessed 6 May 2021).

Department for Education (DfE) (2019) *Understanding Scaled Scores at Key Stage 2* [Online]. Available at: https://www.gov.uk/guidance/understanding-scaled-scores-at-key-stage-2 (Accessed 5 May 2021).

Education Endowment Foundation (n.d.) Assessing and monitoring pupil performance [Online]. Available at: https://educationendowmentfoundation.org.uk/tools/assessing-and-monitoring-pupil-progress/testing/standardised-tests/using-standardised-tests-for-measuring-pupil-progress/ (Accessed 6 May 2021).

Koretz, D. (2009) *Measuring Up*. Cambridge, MA: Harvard University Press (p. 50).

National Foundation for Educational Research (NFER) (2018) The reception baseline assessment [Online]. Available at: www.nfer.ac.uk/media/2837/the-reception-baseline-assessment.pdf (Accessed 6 May 2021).

National Foundation for Educational Research (n.d.) An introduction to standardised scores [Online]. Available at: www.nfer.ac.uk/for-schools/free-resources-advice/assessment-hub/introduction-to-assessment/an-introduction-to-standardised-scores/ (Accessed 5 May 2021).

National Foundation for Educational Research (n.d.) Ask the expert: Interpreting standardised scores with NFER's Liz Twist [Online]. Available at: www.nfer.ac.uk/for-schools/free-resources-advice/assessment-hub/introduction-to-assessment/ask-the-expert-interpreting-standardised-scores/ (Accessed 5 May 2021).

Standards and Testing Agency (2016) Reception baseline comparability study: Results of the 2015 study [Online]. Available at: https://assets.publishing.service.gov.uk/government/uploads/system/uploads/attachment_data/file/514581/Reception_baseline_comparability_study.pdf (Accessed 5 May 2021).

Tidd, M (2018) *Standardised and Scaled Scores* [Online]. Available at: https://michaelt1979.wordpress.com/2018/03/09/standardised-and-scaled-scores/ (Accessed 5 May 2021).

Twist, L. (2018) Interpreting the outcomes of standardised tests [Online]. Available at: www.headteacher-update.com/best-practice-article/interpreting-the-outcomes-of-standardised-tests/182940/ (Accessed 5 May 2021).

TEACHER
ASSESSMENT

5.1   Introduction

Teaching in the British tradition requires an assessment of a student or class's current position within the domain of knowledge being taught; we need to know roughly what a child knows and can do, in order to design and deliver effective opportunities for learning to take place. This type of assessment is somewhat different from the relative-position-amongst-peers ranking assessment for which standardised assessment is best suited. This chapter focuses on assessments made by teachers based on their experience working with those they teach.

Teacher assessment as a term has been increasingly complicated by the requirement for schools to submit teacher assessments which are used within the accountability framework; the Early Years Foundation Stage Profile, Phonics Screening Check and Key Stage 1 assessments are all teacher assessments rather than standardised tests. Some statutory teacher assessments are made using information from written tests, as in Key Stage 1, whereas others rely on teachers or teaching teams' judgements of a student's current performance.

As those who have worked in the classroom will know only too well, managing this kind of assessment is a hugely complex task. Assessment is often further complicated by a child's age; whereas older students can be expected to have developed an understanding of the need to focus on and internalise the information within the curriculum, younger students need a very different approach to help them to learn not only the curriculum content, but the ways in which to learn the curriculum that has been planned for them.

Following the introduction of the national curriculum in the 1990s, the school system became increasingly focused on systems of assessment which aimed to assess whether pupils were learning the things they were expected to learn. At primary level, this led to an extreme form of criterion-based assessment known as Assessing Pupil Progress (APP), which involved teachers making judgements about children's knowledge, skills and understanding against long and detailed lists of learning objectives. In the 2010s, this tick-box approach to assessment faced mounting criticism due to unintended consequences in terms of time and effort that it demanded of teaching staff. It became increasingly apparent that the low levels of reliability and validity of teacher assessment made much of the information of questionable accuracy, and the requirement to make these kinds of judgements began to be phased out.

| Box 5.1 | # Removing objective-level tracking at Stanley Road Primary School: A case study |

Andrew Percival, Deputy Headteacher, Stanley Road Primary School, Oldham

Monitoring children's attainment of individual learning objectives seemed like a great idea at the time but since abandoning the practice, we haven't looked back.

After the publication of the national curriculum in 2014, we asked teachers to record how pupils were progressing with the key objectives for the core subjects of maths, reading and writing. Each year, teachers would diligently review the 30+ objectives for those subjects and indicate the extent to which each pupil had 'achieved' the objective. This data was expected to be filled in on a half-termly basis and, therefore, amounted to around 16,000 individual judgements a year for each teacher. To attempt to reduce the workload burden we encouraged staff to update this on an ongoing basis to avoid having an unmanageable task at the end of each half term. This unwieldy dataset gave us a reassuring sense of instilling order over the messy process of learning. Needless to say, it was all an elaborate illusion taking hundreds of hours of valuable teachers' time to maintain.

We slowly realised that this data was not the robust assessment of each pupil's unique attainment that we were hoping for but merely a house built on sand. Each of those thousands of judgements did not capture the invisible process of *learning* but instead were a record of the visible *performance* in lessons. In other words, we were basing assessment judgements on how many questions pupils were getting right in a particular lesson rather than on whether they had actually learned the content so that they would still be

(Continued)

able to recall it six months or a year later. Psychologists Nick Soderstrom and Robert Bjork describe this as the 'learning–performance distinction'. In fact, Bjork's research on 'desirable difficulties' in 1994 suggested that those pupils who struggled to get to grips with new content in lessons might not perform as well in class in the short term but may be more likely to be able to recall this later on. The struggle helps pupils to remember content, but it doesn't necessarily help the accuracy of your tracker data!

We also began to recognise that many of the objectives we were attempting to track were so broad or vaguely phrased as to be practically meaningless. This was particularly the case with reading objectives where statements such as 'be able to predict what might happen next in a story' appeared in multiple year groups. We realised that a pupil's ability to 'achieve this' depended in no small part on the level of difficulty of the book being read and the background knowledge that the pupil had of the content of the book. What did this look like in Year 3 compared to Year 4? What did a good prediction look like when reading Grimms' fairy tales compared to a reading of Beowulf? We didn't really know but it certainly didn't stop us treating this spurious data as if it were gold dust!

After many months of deliberation, we made the decision to stop assessing individual objectives in this way. Although we were anxious about this, we felt assured that we already had different systems in place that would give teachers the assessment information they needed. Two of these were…

1. Whole class feedback

   In school we use 'whole class feedback' books on a daily basis to record qualitative data about pupils' learning. Brief notes are made in these books after each lesson to record teachers' observations regarding how well pupils understood the content and any common misconceptions and errors that became apparent during the lesson. Instead of providing written marking comments in pupils' books, we then use these notes to feedback verbally to the whole class or to individuals the following day. This feedback is coupled with explicit teaching to help pupils address any errors and gain a better understanding of the lesson content. These 'feedback books' contain a wealth of information concerning how pupils are getting on with learning the curriculum content. This was more useful for teachers to help them adapt their planning and teaching rather than the convoluted recording of numbers on the tracker spreadsheet.

2. Ongoing quizzing of curriculum content

   We improved our existing systems of regular quizzing in the classroom to ensure that any gaps in knowledge were picked up by teachers and acted upon quickly. Quizzes that checked learning from previous units of work alongside more recently taught content were built into daily teaching. We wanted pupils to have multiple opportunities to retrieve what they had been taught in order to strengthen their recall and disrupt the process of forgetting. This felt like a more productive way for teachers to spend their time in identifying and addressing any gaps in learning.

Although we had good intentions with our objective-level tracking, in practice it was an insatiable monster that we haven't missed since we laid it to rest a number of years ago. Teachers are happier, they spend more time thinking about their classroom practice and pupils are still learning as much as they ever did.

The key question for teacher assessment, as with much else in assessing pupils, is to ask what it is that we want to know. Understanding what information we are seeking (and considering what we intend to do with the information) helps us to focus on what we should assess and how we should assess it. Rather than placing children in rank order (which standardised tests do well, as outlined in Chapter 4), teacher assessment often seeks to diagnose which areas of the curriculum pupils have and have not mastered – it is used diagnostically rather than with the aim of ranking.

Teachers can't see into children's heads, so we have to observe what pupils can do through well-designed tasks and written low-stakes assessments. As noted above, we need to assess where we think children currently are in their learning in order to be able to design opportunities for them to learn what we want them to. Effective teacher assessment takes into account the strengths and limitations of our ability to make judgements about those we teach.

As we noted in Chapter 3, the uncertainty surrounding assessment means that whilst we can broadly say whether a pupil is currently in the middle or to the sides of the distribution of their peers, accurate assessment – particularly numerical assessment – is questionable. Furthermore, there are issues with accuracy both in the middle and at the sides of any distribution. Teacher assessment should aim to identify which pupils are broadly in the middle making good development through the curriculum, and those to the sides who are not – particularly those children who need support to access the curriculum. Where pupils are working below or above those typical for their age, teacher assessments can inform the types of actions which might be taken to put additional support in place for those who need it.

As with Chapter 4, this chapter is based around a series of frequently asked questions. These work through the school system in roughly age order, as the questions asked by those teaching the youngest pupils are materially different from those asked by those teaching older teenagers. Additionally, those teaching older students should have access to a wider range of data generated earlier in the student's journey through school, which allows teachers to ask different questions of their assessments.

5.2 Frequently asked questions about teacher assessment

In this section we will have a look at some of the most frequently asked questions about teacher assessment.

5.2.1 Why shouldn't we simply rely on teacher assessment rather than standardised tests?

There are several issues when it comes to relying solely on teacher assessment to assess students. The most import issues are time, accuracy and bias.

Teacher assessment is frequently extremely time consuming. As education has become more centralised, with national curriculums and assessment frameworks, teachers are often asked to assess children against lists of criteria such as those found within the Early Years Foundation Stage Profile (EYFSP), checklists for assessing writing in primary school or level descriptors in Key Stage 3. Where schools use a numerical system to record teacher-assessed attainment, judgements are often standardised in a form which requires teachers to assess against set criteria. Teacher assessments are then frequently moderated by others, requiring further time and effort.

A number of factors work against the accuracy of teacher assessment. Where assessment is based on written criteria, individual interpretation of criteria introduces error as different practitioners and settings interpret texts differently, which is why complex moderation programmes tend to develop in an attempt to standardise judgements. Furthermore, teacher assessments are generally based on observations of student performance rather than embedded student knowledge, which brings into question the accuracy of assessment based on observation.

Human judgement is, unfortunately, inherently biased. Whilst it is possible to try to mitigate bias by developing increased awareness of positive bias, this in itself may introduce negative bias. Attempts to reduce bias tend to require increased time, effort and standardisation, all of which beg the question – if this is the case, why not use standardised assessment rather than teacher assessment?

Teacher assessment is most likely to be effective when it is used alongside independent data on students' performance; a mixture of teacher assessment and standardised assessment is the most efficient method of identifying those students (and cohorts) who need additional support.

5.2.2 How do we best assess children before they can read?

Assessing the youngest children we educate is a highly skilled task, as this can *only* be done by observing children in person. Children who have not learned to read are clearly unable to access a written test independently. Whilst tests for children who have not learned to read have been developed, they rely on an adult working with a child and either recording or assisting children to record responses.

In many cases, assessments of the youngest children are entirely focused on performance against a set of pre-existing criteria. This kind of assessment is generally labelled Criterion-Based Assessment to distinguish it from the Norm-Referenced Assessment of standardised testing, although it may also be referred to as 'descriptor-based assessment' or some variation based on the two terms.

Since the introduction of the Early Years Foundation Stage Profile in the early 2000s, which instituted statutory requirements for schools to report on a number of areas of learning and early learning goals, much of the criteria used to assess young children in England has been standardised across the schools sector. National- or state-level descriptors are increasingly common in many jurisdictions and have had a similar effect to that seen in England, which is that many settings create huge checklists requiring practitioners to record hundreds of different judgements for each child in their care, often alongside photographic proof to corroborate observations.

In England, the toll this has taken on those working with young children is clear in the Pre-School Learning Alliance's *Mind Matters* report of 2018, in which many respondents reported, 'over recent years, the level of paperwork that they are required to complete has steadily increased but that much of it is little more than a "tick-box" exercise which has little to no beneficial impact on children's learning and development' (Pre-School Learning Alliance (PSLA), 2018: 16).

Since 2016, much has been done to attempt to reduce the impact on workload which the most bureaucratic interpretation of the requirements of the EYFS profile had within schools, with the DfE having to include guidance within the EYFS profile handbook on reducing workload. Even with changes to the EYFS profile introduced in 2021, the guidance that settings are 'not required or expected to carry out other assessments in addition to the EYFS profile' (DfE, 2020: 14) and the workload involved in submitting the profile to the DfE has tended to mean that, in practice, the profile *is* the curriculum for the Early Years and continues to drive a great deal of practice in assessing young children.

So, how should we best assess young children before they can read? We suggest that in order to dataproof Early Years, settings should generate a mixture of recorded observations linked to set criteria agreed by those working within the organisation. Whilst these criteria are likely to be closely informed by the EYFS profile, it is important to use the guidance now contained within the handbook, particularly that in section 2.4, 'Evidence and documentation of the EYFS profile' (p. 16), which draws upon 'Eliminating unnecessary workload associated with Data management' (DfE, 2016):

> Over the course of the year, practitioners should build their knowledge of what each child knows and can do. This will help them to make an accurate end of year judgement. They are not required or expected to carry out other assessments in addition to the EYFS profile. Settings can record children's learning in any way that helps practitioners to support their learning and development and make accurate summative assessments.

> Practitioners must make their final EYFS profile assessments based on all their evidence. 'Evidence' means any material, knowledge of the child, anecdotal incident or result of observation, or information from additional sources that supports the overall picture of a child's development.

> Evidence should come from day-to-day activity in the classroom and can be drawn from a variety of sources. The type of evidence will vary from setting to setting, class to class, and even child to child. The form of evidence supporting a practitioner judgement is entirely up to the practitioner. Practitioners should avoid excessive evidence gathering.

> There is no requirement that evidence should be formally recorded or documented. Practitioners should keep paperwork to the minimum needed to illustrate, support and recall their knowledge of the child's attainment.

> A setting's assessment policy should outline when it is necessary to record evidence. In developing their policies, settings should consider how to minimise practitioner workload so they can focus their efforts on teaching.

> When evidence does need to be recorded, this should follow the principles and recommendations outlined in the independent report: Eliminating unnecessary workload associated with data management.

> Practitioners may include the following to support their judgements:

> - knowledge of the child
> - materials, which illustrate the child's learning journey, such as photographs
> - observations of day-to-day interactions
> - video, tape, audio or electronic recordings
> - the child's view of his or her own learning
> - information from parents or other relevant adults.

As we note in Chapter 1, any data which is gathered and collated centrally should – following intelligent analysis and summation – lead to actions for pupils, classes and cohorts. Whilst EYFS data has to be gathered and collated in order to complete the statutory requirement to report children's development in the reception year, a dataproof school should use the framework to direct effort by establishing as quickly as possible those children who are likely to thrive without any additional support.

Once this broad group has been identified, settings should focus on gathering appropriate data for those children who have been identified as needing additional support. Once this data has been analysed, and support has been agreed and begun to be implemented – this is likely to happen during the autumn term for September starters – the children who are expected to make appropriate progress can be assessed in groups, allowing efficient gathering of data to support teacher assessments.

As children move into Year 1 and are increasingly able to decode text but are often unable to independently access written assessments, the same broad principles apply: focus effort on those children who need support to make the development which is reasonably expected of children in Year 1, whilst minimising the data collation workload.

When it comes to assessing reading itself, in these early stages of reading teachers are mostly tasked with assessing children's ability to decode written language. The statutory Year 1 Phonics Screening Check (PSC) is based on sound assessment principles: it presents an age- and stage-appropriate task to assess the extent of children's knowledge of phonics; it is time and effort efficient; and it provides information which is independent of the assessor. What is more, the PSC gives a very clear indication of those children who are unlikely to require any additional support to access the Year 1/2 curriculum and those for whom further support is likely to be necessary.

Box 5.2

Why is the Phonics Screening Check designed the way it is?

The PSC consists of forty words which children are asked to decode. Adults who administer the test introduce the check and pupils are given time to practise the mechanics involved. Once the check itself begins, adults must not say or do anything to give children any particular advantage. There are 20 real words and 20 'alien' words, which represent the names of imaginary creatures.

(Continued)

The stipulation that adults should not point to words or indicate how to decode them is intended to eliminate any potential bias, however unintended, on the part of whoever is administering the check.

The inclusion of 'alien' words is to reduce the bias in favour of children with extensive experience of written English, who are likely to have seen and therefore have knowledge of the 'real' words in the check.

The check is in two sections, each consisting of 20 words, to break up the process so that it does not feel too onerous for the child undertaking it. Most of the words have a single syllable; some double-syllable words are included to assess those children working at the higher range of Year 1 reading ability.

The threshold for achieving the expected standard has been set at 32 since the first check in 2012. The vast majority of children score 32 or above, with roughly 80% attaining the expected standard since 2016 (DfE, 2019: 3). The distribution of scores has indicated some bias in the reporting of scores since the check began, with clear anomalies in scores reported as 31 and 32.

5.2.3 How should we assess emerging writers?

As children begin to master writing for an audience, the nature of the assessments that teachers can undertake begins to change. The curriculum begins to focus on key knowledge in reading, writing and maths which the children need to learn and practise using, as well as foundation subjects as laid out in the national curriculum. Rather than simply observing performance by watching what children can do, we can set written tasks for children to undertake – with varying degrees of independence – which allow children to show what they know and can do. As children begin to write, they begin to be able to record their thinking and can provide written answers to questions we set. This introduces more opportunities for us to assess where children are in their learning.

As noted above, we should be clear as to what information we want teachers to assess. A dataproof school will be very careful in its selection of information it asks teachers to gather and collate centrally. Teachers will, of course, gather a great deal from the emerging writers they teach, much of which will not be collated centrally.

Teachers will want to gather information on children's writing in itself. The National Curriculum (DfE, 2013: 10–11) outlines the programme of study which most schools will use for emerging writing; it includes what is expected of pupils' handwriting, transcription and composition.

So, how should we best assess emerging writers? We suggest that to dataproof teacher assessment of early writing, settings should monitor handwriting, transcription and composition.

- **Handwriting:** can be monitored using a simple low-stakes assessment of children's ability to transcribe the alphabet. Pupils should write this from memory where possible; if they have yet to memorise the shapes and sequence of letters, they may need scaffolded support.
- **Transcription:** can be monitored using a simple transcription task. This should be a short text which can be read aloud to children, who then transcribe what they hear.
- **Composition:** by reading their own writing aloud. Emerging writing can be difficult to decipher as children's handwriting and choice of phonemes can be idiosyncratic; it is generally more efficient to ask children to generate their own ideas and then to read them aloud.

We suggest that teaching teams undertake a set of standard tasks in the first or second week of each term. Handwriting can be assessed in a simple whole class task; transcription and composition can be assessed via whole class transcription and composition tasks, followed up by a series of group tasks in which children share their writing by reading aloud.

As usual, pupils should be broadly assessed as either being in need of additional support or developing as expected. This assessment can be done whilst children are undertaking the tasks and should not need additional time to record.

For those children who need additional support, teachers can draw on a broad range of guidance to help them to identify any specific areas of concern. The Education Endowment Foundation's *Improving Literacy in Key Stage 1* (2020: 28–39) is a good source of information; recommendations 5 and 6 focus on writing skills (5 – Teach pupils to use strategies for planning and monitoring their writing; 6 – Promote fluent written transcription skills by encouraging extensive and effective practice and explicitly teaching spelling).

Diagnostic tasks which enable teachers to assess children's transcription, text generation and executive function will enable teaching teams to plan learning opportunities and support of those children who are finding writing difficult. A bank of these tasks should be built up so that tasks can be reused in future.

5.2.4 How should we assess written work?

Assessing written answers to examiners' questions ushered in the modern era of education data. Before written tests, pupils were assessed by interrogating their knowledge and understanding in person ('viva voce', a Latin phrase meaning roughly 'with living voice', which we retain as 'viva' in higher education). Written tests began by replicating the oral questions and soon evolved as the limitations of assessing this kind of written work became clear.

Those limitations are still with us, of course. Skilled candidates can emphasise the positive and the less skilled may miss the subtleties of the question they are being asked to answer. Simple written tests often lack validity as additional factors skew results – pupils with greater life experience generally find writing easier, for example, and younger children may not be inclined to consider what those reading written answers are actually looking for.

Attempts to make the assessment of written work more rigorous have often been steered down a criterion-referenced route in which writing is assessed against sets of standards or expectations. In the early years of the national curriculum and statutory testing in Key Stages 1, 2 and 3, writing was assessed via complex mark schemes which attempted to anticipate answers that pupils might record. As those marking written work often had to make judgements based on the mark schemes, a programme of moderation was generally used in an attempt to stand-ardise judgements.

Despite these attempts to standardise judgements, assessing written work using written tests came under fire, especially at primary level, as was made clear in the Bew Report in 2011 (Bew, 2011: 56). From 2013, external tests assessing writing were discontinued at Key Stage 2. Whilst writing became teacher assessed, there was further controversy in 2016 when teacher assess-ment changed from a 'best fit' model (which included some flexibility in assess-ment) to a 'secure fit' model (in which pupils had to demonstrate competency in all aspects in order to meet expected standards). Following consultation, a degree of flexibility returned to the assessment of writing at Key Stages 1 and 2 (Ofqual, 2019: 11–12).

In Key Stage 3, all external testing was abandoned in 2009, along with the require-ment to provide teacher assessments of attainment (Department for Children, Schools and Families (DCSF), 2009: 1), largely due to a failure in the administra-tion of the 2008 Key Stages 2 and 3 statutory assessments, as well as the criticism of the burden placed on schools.

The criticisms of criterion-based assessment of written work have encouraged the development of alternative methods of assessment, one of the more promising of which is comparative judgement. This attempts to rank pupils based on their written work, rather than to require time-consuming judgements of absolute attain-ment. Many teachers use this method informally to place students' work in approx-imate rank order from least to most advanced; comparative judgement introduces a number of checks and balances to increase the reliability and validity of the judgements which are being made.

> ### Box 5.3   Comparative judgement
>
> Rather than relying on written descriptions of standards, comparative judgement is a method of assessing writing by comparing one piece of writing to another. It is based on the theory that humans are better at making comparisons than making absolute judgements. By combining judgements made by a number of markers to reduce the influence of potential outlier comparisons, a broad ranking of level of attainment can be constructed (Bramley and Vitello, 2016: 43).
>
> Whilst comparative judgement has a history reaching back in the early 20th century, recent developments in computing power have increased interest as it is now much easier to develop systems that allow judgements to be made quickly and efficiently.
>
> In summary, a comparative judgement system requires that pupils are given a straightforward written task. Their answers should be relatively short – a page of A4 is ideal. Their writing is then scanned and uploaded to an online system in a common image format. Judges – generally teachers in schools – are then asked to make comparisons between pieces of work, deciding which of the two items presented on screen is of a higher standard. The process repeats and the result is a national rank order of pupils' writing.
>
> In order to position pupils' writing within the national cohort, some judgement of work by pupils who attend other schools is required in order to integrate judgements. No More Marking, the organisation which has been pioneering comparative judgement in England, does this by asking judges to compare pupils who attend two different external schools.

In this chapter, we focus on teacher assessment of pupils to ascertain which are making good development through the curriculum and which may need additional support. Assessing written work via comparative judgement is particularly effective provided systems are in place to manage the limitations of individual judgements.

In assessing written work, it is essential to establish the aim of the assessment. Is the aim to assess the pupil's ability to write well or to assess knowledge and understanding of the subject? If it is to assess the ability to write well, this should be carefully aligned with the curriculum and the expectations at each stage of the pupil's development. If it is to assess knowledge and understanding of the subject, the focus should be on reducing as far as possible the influence of the ability to write well to ensure that this does not colour judgements. The separation of writing into grammar, spelling and punctuation and composition in Key Stages 1 and 2 and the separation of English into Language and Literature in Key Stages 3 and 4 should help to inform how assessments should be separated.

5.2.5 Teacher assessment of the ability to write well

At primary level, we suggest that pupils are given an extended writing task at the beginning of each year. The task should allow a child to demonstrate their awareness of writing, focusing on grammar, punctuation and spelling. The same task should be undertaken at the end of the academic year (in the third or fourth week before the end of the summer term). A comparison between the two pieces will provide the opportunity to show how a child has developed over the year.

We recommend that your school gathers and collates these tasks centrally, or in a form which ensures that a record of a child's development in writing over time is maintained. Where this record is in place, a comparison with the task the pupil undertook at the beginning of the previous year – or previous years – will allow teachers to identify next steps in the child's learning.

For the majority of a class, the next step is simply to be fully engaged in the curriculum. For those children who clearly need support to develop the necessary age-appropriate knowledge, skills and understanding, an action plan should be put in place to support the child's development. Where possible, the action plan should include areas of development which will be undertaken with the whole of the class, as those for whom there are no particular concerns will certainly benefit from the opportunity to revisit or consolidate previous learning.

For example, if a Year 5 child shows limited awareness of the conventions of using punctuation of direct speech (which would be expected in Year 5), plan to revisit and consolidate this learning with the whole class. Where a child struggles with letter formation in Year 3, plan to address the issues identified with the whole of the class. For issues specific to an individual – where a pupil has struggled to write at the expected length or depth for their age, for example – further diagnostic assessment may be necessary (Chapter 6, in which we look at assessing outliers, may be of help here).

We suggest using similar teacher assessed tasks to assess the ability to write well in secondary schools.

5.2.6 Assessing knowledge and understanding of a subject via written work

Using written work to assess knowledge and understanding is central to much of the ongoing assessment teachers do. It is crucial that any limitations in a pupil's transcriptive aspects of writing do not influence teacher assessments of knowledge and understanding; this is often easier said than done, but an awareness of the potential bias which limited transcription skill may introduce can help its effect. Tasks which require pupils to write extended answers can often result in written work that is difficult to assess, as a pupil's ability to transcribe, compose and manage the task may affect the content of the writing. Extended answers have the advantage that a pupil's work is unlikely to be copied by others, making the sharing or copying of answers less likely.

To counter these issues, teachers may opt to make use of written questions which require shorter, more specific answers. This can be effective in assessing pupils' knowledge of very specific aspects of the curriculum in a given subject but can encourage some children to share or copy answers.

At primary level, to assess subject knowledge and understanding in the foundation subjects, teachers should consider using a limited number of questions which include answers of varying length. The aim of any assessment is to be able to rank the children into three broad categories to indicate those in the middle of the distribution, those who are more advanced and those who need support.

At secondary level, teachers should again aim to broadly rank pupils into a number of categories based on their written work using a limited number of questions which include answers of varying length.

5.2.7 What other data can teachers generate?

Schools collect extensive contextual data (including, but not limited to, Free School Meal Status, dates of birth, start date and so on). Teachers can also make judgements on a wide range of additional factors which help to build a picture of a pupil's experience and needs in school.

Many schools have a system of assessing pupils' attitudes to learning and behaviour. This is usually a simple scale with three to five categories. The categories are often described by a written statement in an effort to bring some degree of consistency to the judgements.

Schools may also record teacher assessments of behaviour, using a similar three- to five-point scale. A judgement of family engagement in supporting learning can also be made.

For some pupils, schools may ask teachers to make a judgement on barriers to learning with a flag to indicate whether the teacher has any concerns or not. Where there are concerns, these can be recorded using simple statements.

These judgements may be shared with or recorded in conjunction with pupils.

Depending on context, there may be additional contextual factors on which teachers can make judgements.

5.2.8 How secure should we expect teacher assessments to be?

As with any system that seeks to make summative judgements, we want teacher assessment to be as accurate and consistent as it can be. After all, if two individuals have very different ideas as to an acceptable standard it can make any comparison difficult. Unfortunately, accuracy and consistency in judgements of individuals is extremely problematic. One temptation is to implement complex moderation systems which often have immense workload costs combined with limited improvement in quality of judgements. A further temptation is to become ever more prescriptive in the criteria for making judgements, which also has workload and motivational costs. Yet another issue is the perverse incentives which a system of teacher assessment often introduces; teachers may be encouraged, however subtly, to moderate judgements based on what they believe is expected of them. Others may simply game the system to their own benefit.

Ultimately, teacher assessments should be seen as one part of the data landscape in school. Putting too much weight on their accuracy and consistency will have negative consequences of one kind or another. Accepting this and making it clear that as a school you understand the wide margins of error inherent in teacher assessment will improve your use of judgements made by your staff.

Ultimately, the key question is how much weight we should put on teacher assessments. There is often a dilemma at the heart of asking teachers to make judgements. What's more, young children may often not co-operate in any assessment of their performance – as those who work with the youngest learners know only too well – making assessment a challenging task.

5.3 Summary

In this chapter, we have looked at teacher assessment and how it is an integral part of the English education system. We have looked at the cost of teacher assessment, particularly in terms of the time teacher assessment can take. Additionally, we have looked at the potential for unintended and unwelcome bias to distort our judgement. We have examined how standardised tests can support our teacher assessments by highlighting any discrepancies in our assumptions.

We have looked at the assessment of children before they can read, as well as considering how best to assess emerging writers and those pupils who are or have become confident writers. We have also considered teacher-generated assessment of contextual factors which may affect pupils as they progress through school.

In addition we have considered how secure we should expect teacher assessment to be, given the detail we have explored in this chapter. The focus of this chapter has been on pupils who are likely to be within the middle of the distribution of their peers; in Chapter 6, we will look at those pupils who we assess to be at the edges of the typical distribution of pupils as we consider those who are outliers within the system.

References

Bew, P. (2011) *Independent Review of Key Stage 2 Testing, Assessment and Accountability*. London: DfE.

Bjork, R.A. (1994) 'Institutional impediments to effective training', in D. Druckman and R.A. Bjork (eds), *Learning, Remembering, Believing: Enhancing human performance*. Washington, DC: National Academy Press.

Bramley, T. and Vitello, S. (2016) 'The effect of adaptivity on the reliability coefficient in adaptive comparative judgement', *Assessment in Education: Principles, Policy & Practice*, 26 (1): 43–58.

Department for Children, Schools and Families (DCSF) (2009) *Explanatory Memorandum to the Education (School Performance Information) (England) (Amendment) Regulations 2009*. London: DCSF.

Department for Education (DfE) (2013) *The National Curriculum in England Key Stages 1 and 2 Framework Document*. London: DfE.

Department for Education (DfE) (2016) *Eliminating Unnecessary Workload Associated with Data Management*. London: DfE.

Department for Education (DfE) (2019) *Phonics Screening Check and Key Stage 1 Assessments in England, 2019*. London: DfE.

Department for Education (DfE) (2020) *Early Years Foundation Stage Profile 2021 Handbook*. London: DfE.

Education Endowment Foundation (EEF) (2020) *Improving Literacy in Key Stage 1*. London: EEF.

Ofqual (2019) *A Review of Approaches to Assessing Writing at the End of Primary Education*. London: Ofqual.

Pre-School Learning Alliance (PSLA) (2018) *Minds Matter*. London: PSLA.

Soderstrom, N.C. and Bjork R.A. (2015) 'Learning versus performance: An integrative review', *Perspectives on Psychological Science*, 10 (2): 176–99.

OUTLIERS

What you will learn from this chapter:

- The issues of collecting, analysing and reporting data relating to pupils working below curriculum expectations
- What data you should and should not collect about such pupils
- The importance of provision mapping for pupils with special educational needs
- An overview of the challenges of assessing pupils working well above expectations

6.1   A question of scale

We can think of the data a school records as a series of maps at varying scales, and we select the appropriate scale according to the needs of the pupils we aim to support. Smaller scale maps give us a wider view over a larger area; larger scale maps provide the detail of a specific area we want to focus on. In its broadest sense, assessment will commonly group pupils according to whether they are working below, within or above expectations and this will generate a small-scale map of standards across the school, which is adequate for, say, reporting to governors. For those pupils that are keeping pace with the curriculum – that teachers have few concerns about – there may not be a requirement to go beyond such a general assessment. If a pupil is fine, do we need to record more than a test score each term or even a teacher's judgement annually? It is when pupils are struggling that schools may need to make more regular assessments to build a more detailed picture over time; and pupils that are working well above and below curriculum expectations are those for whom the most information is required. The types of assessment that work for the majority may not be appropriate here. Instead, schools need to find more suitable and insightful methods that allow them to zoom in and build that larger scale map of learning. This chapter discusses the data that schools do and do not need to collect, with a particular focus on detailed provision mapping for pupils with special educational needs.

6.2 Assessment and support for pupils working well below curriculum expectations

Many schools, especially primary schools where most pupils are working through the same curriculum at the same pace towards the same national standards, are opting for a simple system of teacher assessment. This usually involves classifying pupils as working either towards, within or above expectations depending on how well they are coping with what is being taught at any given point. Such summative assessments can easily be compared to prior results or future targets – using a simple matrix for example (see Chapter 7) – to identify groups of pupils that are falling behind or making good progress.

In secondary schools, especially at Key Stage 3 where it is inappropriate to use GCSE grades, summative assessment is less straightforward as pupils may be in different sets for certain subjects and therefore working at different levels. What constitutes expectations therefore varies according to the set the pupil is in, and schools may seek to adopt a system that indicates both the pupil's security within what is being taught and the level it is being taught at. This solves the problem of pupils in lower sets that are meeting expectations appearing to be above those pupils in the higher sets that are classified as working towards expectations. It is certainly difficult – perhaps impossible – to devise a common approach that works sufficiently well across all phases and key stages of education.

All systems of assessment and classification are imperfect, constantly evolving, and far from resolved in many schools, but they are coalescing towards something resembling those described above. The best advice is to keep things simple, meaningful, communicable and – as far as is reasonably practicable – free from the distorting effects of accountability. As discussed in previous chapters, schools should also avoid the distraction of the pursuit of progress measures, which lead schools to invent hierarchical systems of ladders and flightpaths and reduce assessment to a numbers game. By aiming for simplicity and clarity and steering clear of unsubstantiated and abstract series of levels, we can devise systems that work for the majority of pupils in a school.

There is, of course, a 'but'. As stated, we can devise systems that work for the majority of pupils: most teachers seem happy – and tend to agree that it makes sense – to simply assess pupils as working towards, within or above expectations. The wheels of the system begin to wobble, however, when we apply it to pupils that are not accessing the same curriculum as their peers, who are working a year or more below 'age-related' expectations or perhaps are even working below the standards of the current educational phase. Systems that work well for the majority of pupils often fall short when it comes to pupils with special educational needs and disabilities (SEND).

Understandably, teachers are opposed to systems that classify pupils with SEND as 'below' at each assessment point, and such clumsy terminology is unlikely to go down well with parents. In order to avoid this issue of pupils getting stuck in the below band for the duration of their education – which is a depressing prospect – schools will often resort to devising additional categories of assessment that sit alongside or are appended to the main set of assessments. This will commonly involve a series of bands that supposedly represent the 'small steps' of progress made by those with SEND that are working below expectations. It is now common for schools in England to have just three summative assessment categories to accommodate the vast majority of pupils – those working within expectations – but many more categories for the small number of pupils with SEND that are working below. When asked why these steps are needed, teachers will often say that they 'have to show the progress', but to whom it is unclear. Most worryingly, these steps may lack strict criteria, leaving assessment open to interpretation or even guesswork.

It is common for the school's system of tracking to be underpinned by an expectation that pupils with SEND make a certain number of steps per year without ever clearly defining what a step is. The notion of measuring small steps is well intended, but what actually are they? One child's small step can be another's giant leap. Unlike a watt, joule or newton, a small step is not a standard unit of measurement. Once again, progress measures become the tail that wags the dog.

For many years, a series of P Scales has been used in English schools to assess pupils with special educational needs working below the level of the statutory national assessments (Department for Education, 2017). Over time, it became increasingly common for P Scales to be adopted more widely, for the purposes of interim assessments made between the statutory points, and inevitably they were incorporated into school tracking systems. Following the Rochford Review in 2016, it was decided that P Scales would be replaced by a new system of assessment, and it is worth bearing in mind that the reasons given for their removal are almost identical to those given for the removal of Levels. P Scales had come to be seen as a progression model: they gave the impression that progress was linear, that pupils moved through them at a fixed rate. Worse still, in an effort to show progress over shorter periods, schools divided P Scales into subunits that were defined by little more than a wet finger raised to the wind. Even now, schools in pursuit of funding for pupils with SEND are confronted with forms that ask for numerical proxies of progress. In need of the money, some numbers are entered into the boxes on the form – not too high, not too low – and fingers are crossed that the application is successful.

The notion that any pupil makes linear progress through a curriculum is clearly flawed, but it is especially misguided when dealing with pupils with SEND whose educational journeys are individual and tailored to meet their needs. It is, therefore, imperative that – regardless of internal impetus or external pressure – we avoid systems that, contrary to all evidence, suggest pupils with SEND progress at the same rate. We need systems that work for all pupils, that present an accurate picture of learning, not just of pupils working at 'age-related' expectations, but of those working below, too. We need to recognise that there is no one-size-fits-all approach to assessment: what works for one pupil may not work for another, and we should seek out more appropriate methods that provide us with actionable information.

To dataproof your school, you need better data.

6.2.1 Recording assessment of pupils working below curriculum expectations

Teacher assessment is the most valuable tool in the assessment toolbox, and this is most certainly the case when it comes to pupils with SEND who may struggle to access mainstream tests. But what data can we collect that is useful? As mentioned, continually recording pupils as 'working below' is too broad to give any impression of progress, tells us nothing useful, and is demoralising when reported to parents. Schools seeking to circumvent this problem will often take one of two routes:

1. **Record how many years below the pupil is working**. This results in assessment data along the lines of B-1, B-2 and so on, where B indicates that the pupil is working below, and the negative number expresses that as a number of years. Some schools have taken this further with decimals to indicate the proportion of a year that the pupil is working below their age-appropriate curriculum. This results in bandings such as B-1.5 and B-2.3, which supposedly tell us that the pupil is working one and a half or two and a third years below. Inevitably, the band assigned to the pupil at a previous assessment point is subtracted from that assigned at the latest point to give a numerical expression of progress. All too often, such bandings are not based on any form of standardised assessment; they are instead highly likely to be derived from the proportion of a previous year's learning objectives that the pupil has secured at the assessment point in question. This approach will result in far more assessment categories for pupils with SEND than for other pupils.

2. **State the year's curriculum the pupil is working within**. There may be value in recording that a pupil in, say Year 5, is working within the Year 2 curriculum.

Typically, however, schools will attempt to be more definitive by indicating where in that year's curriculum the child is working or how securely they are working within it. Unfortunately, the approach taken and the message the data is supposed to convey are not always obvious, and this is particularly the case where terms such as 'emerging', 'developing' and 'secure' have been appended to the year indicator. We may therefore see a Year 5 pupil classified as Y2D (Year 2 Developing) or Y3E (Year 3 Emerging). In some schools, these terms are intended to denote the pupil's security in that particular year's curriculum at a given point in time; in other schools, it might simply refer to the proportion of that year's curriculum that the pupil has covered, where 'emerging' equates to the first term's teaching, and so on. Such terms are therefore ambiguous and their application non-standardised. Invariably, point scores are assigned to each increment and, as above, a previous assessment will be subtracted from the latest one to provide a progress score. Schools that adopt this approach usually use the same continuous, linear scale for all pupils. It is, essentially, a rebadged version of the old system of sublevels that was discontinued in English schools in 2015.

In both the above cases, the driving force behind the approach is a desire or need – depending on the vulnerability of the school – to measure progress. The first example is designed to only measure the progress of pupils with SEND who will move up through the 'working below' bands over time; other pupils will generally be assessed as working towards, within or above expectations and will often remain in the same category from one term – or year – to the next. The second example places pupils with SEND on the same scale as all other pupils so that a Year 5 pupil with SEND that progresses through the Year 2 curriculum receives the same progress score as a Year 5 pupil that is keeping pace with the age-appropriate, Year 5 curriculum. This implies that the progress of these two hypothetical children – one with SEND and working three years below, and the other working within the age-appropriate curriculum – have made equal and comparable progress. But is that really the case? Have these two children made the same amount of progress or have they both made 'good' progress but in very different and incomparable ways?

There are even cases where schools have added 'below' and 'above' to the year indicator, which is even more nonsensical. The Year 5 pupil that is working in the Year 2 curriculum could, therefore, be described as 'Year 2 Below' or 'Year 2 Above'. But doesn't that imply that the pupil is actually working in the Year 1 or Year 3 curriculum?

All these approaches are a fudge to provide the comfort of neat and convenient progress metrics to keep external agencies, governors and parents happy. But they lack rigour and are too prone to distortion. As mentioned above, the common response to the question 'why do this?' is 'we have to show progress'. In such a scenario, schools may feel compelled to engineer systems that give the right impression to those with oversight, whereby teachers place pupils into a lower band at the start of the year and higher band at the end, and the tracking system dutifully provides the right number on the graph. This issue is especially pertinent to pupils with SEND for whom many schools are clearly under pressure to generate data that supposedly 'proves' the progress they make.

6.2.2 Criteria-based assessment

If schools decide to track the progress of pupils with SEND through a series of age-related bands, how do they decide which band those pupils are in? Often this will come down to criteria- (or descriptor-) based assessment: a checklist of statements against which the pupil's learning is compared (Christodoulou, 2016). It is common for pupils with SEND to be referenced against statements that relate to an earlier year group's curriculum so that, in the example above, the Year 5 pupil would be assessed against Year 2 criteria. The percentage of statements checked off the list and the pupil's security within those aspects will define their position within that year's curriculum. This is a common activity in schools and is the main engine that powers the generation of summative assessment in various popular tracking systems.

There are several problems with this process:

1. **The self-fulfilling prophesy**: once a teacher has decided to track the Year 5 pupil against a Year 2 criteria, it is a foregone conclusion that the pupil will be classified as working within Year 2.
2. **Inconsistent interpretations**: the criteria are often very broad and can be interpreted in different ways. There is a risk that the expectations applied to the pupil with SEND may not be as high as those for whom the criteria are 'age-related'.
3. **Workload**: the process of checking learning against a list of statements can be extremely laborious.
4. **Bias**: judgements against criteria are prone to bias.

The question here is not whether criteria-based assessment should be used. Despite the issues outlined above it is common practice in many subjects and is the main method of assessment in primary education in England where government-produced frameworks are used to guide assessment in the Early Years, at Key Stage 1 (age 7), and in writing at Key Stage 2 (age 11). The question is: should schools attempt to collect data at this level of detail and, if they do, what value will that data provide? As mentioned, one of the key issues with this process of criteria-based assessment is workload: teachers may spend hours checking pupils' activities against the lists of criteria in order to arrive at a judgement. Often these checklists will be stored in electronic form in the school's tracking system, where they will be scored and colour-coded on a regular, or even continual, basis. The fear is that upon realising the stark inappropriateness of comparing a pupil with SEND against criteria relating to an earlier year's curriculum, the teacher or special needs coordinator (SENDCO) will set about devising checklists for each support strategy, thus ramping up the workload even further. As with all data collection, schools need to have honest conversations about whether collecting data at criterion level – for example, judgements made against each curriculum statement – is beneficial. As always, we need to be mindful of the impact on learning versus the impact on workload. We must also consider whether anyone is ever going to look at the data we collect and, if they do, will it tell them anything they didn't already know?

In other words, do the ends justify the means?

6.2.3 What data should schools collect?

In a dataproof school there are no arbitrary age bands to measure the progress of children working below curriculum expectations. Such schools will have considered the motivations behind data collection and re-evaluated the benefit of collecting and storing detailed data at criteria level. But if we let go of the 'small steps' of progress and minutiae of tracking statements, what is left?

When it comes to pupils with SEND, what data is useful?

The rest of this section aims to answer this question by focusing on five main areas:

- Group-level reporting
- Standardised assessments
- Gap analysis
- Engagement
- Provision mapping.

Box 6.1

Can we measure the effectiveness of interventions?

At many points in this chapter, and elsewhere in this book, we mention monitoring the effectiveness of interventions. This is desirable because schools want to demonstrate that the additional support they provide for pupils – often those with SEND – is working and offers value for money, and such information is likely to be reported to governors and external agencies. But we have to acknowledge an important point here: it's just not that straightforward. First, as discussed in previous chapters, data is noisy and, in the case of teacher assessment, prone to bias. Second, the amount of progress that is deemed 'expected' will most likely vary from pupil to pupil and so there is no common benchmark. And third, to truly measure the effectivess of an intervention strategy, we need to establish control groups. That may be a requirement of a clinical trial but it's just not feasible (or fair!) in an education setting. And could we ever hope to control for all the variables anyway? We can, therefore, infer something about effectiveness from the data, but we can never be absolutely certain the strategies we employ are responsible for the improvements we see.

6.2.3.1 Group-level reporting

This refers to aggregated data – summarised to group level – that schools may be required to prepare for audiences such as boards of governors or external advisors. Such data compares the attainment and progress of one group of children against another; and is intended to reveal areas of relative underperformance that need to be addressed. One of these key groups is, of course, children with SEND.

Logically, this topic should be last on the list because it cannot be resolved until the pupil-level data has been collected. There are, however, huge problems with attempting to draw inferences from group-level data due to the often small number of pupils, the overlap between groups, and the skew caused by outliers. It is, therefore, highly unlikely that such data is telling audiences what they might think it is telling them, and this is especially true when it comes to pupils with SEND. The risk of false conclusion is high and, as always, schools must avoid allowing misguided demands to influence their assessment strategy.

Comparing the performance of pupils with SEND to those without is clearly pointless, no matter how inconvenient this is to those requesting such data. Nor should one pupil with SEND be compared against another, or the school 'SEND group' as a whole be compared against supposedly more equitable SEND national averages.

> Because of the often vastly different types of pupils' needs, inspectors will not compare the outcomes achieved by pupils with SEND with those achieved by other pupils with SEND in the school, locally or nationally. (Ofsted, 2021)

At the time of writing, Ofsted is not presenting attainment or progress data for the SEND group of pupils in the Inspection Data Summary Report (IDSR), choosing instead to simply provide a contextual summary of the numbers of pupils in each of the main categories of SEND. This is useful information about the school community. Perhaps then we could compare the performance of pupils grouped by type of SEND, of which there are twelve collected via the school census (Department for Education, 2021). This is more definitive and therefore meaningful, but the same problems persist: small numbers, overlap, skew. And even if there were enough pupils to allow for statistically valid analysis, there can be huge variation even within a single category of SEND.

SEND is not a homogenous group, and to treat pupils with SEND as such for reporting purposes is a mistake. It does not tell anyone anything useful. Instead, data should remain at the individual level if it is to inform meaningful discussion. This is problematic when reporting to governors and the like who should not have sight of names, but we can present the number of pupils with SEND in each year group, perhaps broken down by SEND category so the broad spectrum of need is more evident. It is then incumbent on those scrutinising the data to enquire about the adequacy of provision that has been put in place to meet the needs of pupils, some of whom may have multiple and complex needs. Are we satisfied with the support provided for that particular child? Are they well served by this school? How do we monitor the effectiveness of our additional support and interventions? Should we be doing anything differently? These are more useful conversations than tracking the attainment gap between the SEND group and their peers or national average.

There is perhaps one area where we might consider aggregating data and that relates to the support strategies a school provides. The example of a provision map shown in section 6.2.3.5 includes summary rows, which document the change in average reading ages over time. These could be used to inform discussions about the effectiveness of additional support.

6.2.3.2 Standardised assessment

A problem that many schools face is that pupils with SEND often struggle to access the age-recommended suite of tests taken by their peers, and attempts result in very low to zero scores. To get round this – as with criteria-based assessment – a common approach is to administer tests intended for earlier year groups. This, on the face of it, seems logical, and if your intention is to find out, say, how much of the Year 2 maths curriculum the Year 5 pupil understands, then this may be a suitable method. But it will not fulfil the main function of a standardised test, which is to tell us whereabouts in the national population of similarly aged children the pupil ranks. It will instead tell us where this 9- or 10-year-old child ranks amongst pupils aged 6 to 7 years old. Therefore, the Year 5 pupil that takes a Year 2 test and achieves a standardised score of 82 – representing the 12th percentile – is not in the lowest 12 percent of Year 5 pupils; they are in the lowest 12% of Year 2 pupils. It is questionable whether that information is in any way useful. It is also worth noting that it is far less common for schools to administer tests intended for older year groups to their highest attaining pupils. This is either because it hasn't crossed their mind to do so, or because they'd rather have the higher scores the pupil would inevitably achieve by taking the age-appropriate test.

In addition to using tests designed for earlier years, schools that administer standardised tests each term – common practice in many settings – will generally use the test that matches the current term. For example, during the autumn term, whilst most Year 5 pupils are taking the age-appropriate autumn test – as intended – the pupil with SEND is required to sit the Year 2 autumn test instead. This again seems logical because it is, after all, autumn. But would it not be more useful to assess that pupil using the end of year test to ascertain how secure they are in the entire Year 2 curriculum rather than just a part of it?

These are common mistakes made by schools wanting to use standardised tests to assess pupils with SEND that are working below curriculum expectations. We need to understand and accept that what works for the majority may not work for all, and when it comes to pupils with SEND, there are more appropriate, diagnostic methods of standardised assessment that are worth exploring. These tests will be more efficient, accurate and will provide actionable information. Such tests usually produce reading, spelling and maths ages, which – whilst just a different way of presenting standardised data – are easier to understand and therefore a good option for reporting results to parents. Alternatives to fixed, paper-based, curriculum-linked standardised tests include:

Parallel tests

Unlike the serial tests commonly used in schools, which link to the curriculum, build in difficulty from one test to the next, and are intended to be administered at specific points in time, parallel tests are designed for repeat testing and are comparable in difficulty. They are therefore useful for assessing the effectiveness of additional support put in place for children with SEND and can be used more flexibly than termly tests. As with other types of test, these generate standardised scores and age assessments.

Adaptive tests

As discussed in Chapter 4, these differ from the 'fixed' type of tests commonly used in schools in which all pupils are confronted with the same set of questions. Such tests can present significant barriers to pupils with special educational needs, which may lead schools to administer earlier years' tests with all the problems that brings. In an adaptive test, on the other hand, the questions posed depend on the answers given previously, and the child is routed through the test, tackling questions that quickly settle at an appropriate level of challenge. These tests are therefore better suited to pupils with special educational needs – they are quicker and do not require a pupil to face pages of questions that are beyond their capability. Paper format versions are available, but the nature of such tests lends itself to a computer-based approach. Again, adaptive tests will provide results in the form of standardised scores and age equivalents.

Comparative judgement

As discussed in Chapter 5, comparative judgement is an alternative to criteria-based assessment and a suitable option for those subjects such as writing where no standardised test is available. Samples of pupils' writing are compared and ranked against other pupils' work, both in school and – if using a system such as No More Marking – nationally. In addition to a rank score, this can also provide writing ages and standardised scores, which will sit alongside the other assessment data derived from standardised tests stored in your assessment database.

6.2.3.3 Gap analysis

Gap analysis tends to have two meanings. First, there is the comparison of the results of various groups of pupils over time to monitor whether the gap between them is widening or narrowing. This is usually expressed as an average score or percentage. In England there is a focus on the attainment gap between disadvantaged pupils – those eligible for Free School Meals at any point in the last six years, or those in care or adopted from care – and other pupils. Whilst this is still a national priority – once branded 'closing the gap', then a more cautious 'narrowing the gap', which briefly became the alliterative 'diminishing the difference' – it tends to be analysed at national or area level rather than at school level where numbers are often small and 'apparent differences [between groups] are often likely to be statistical noise' (Spielman, 2018).

Gap analysis of this type spiralled out of control in the days of RAISEonline – the DfE's now defunct school data analysis tool – when schools were regularly interrogated about the performance gaps between a bewildering number of groups, some of which contained just a handful of pupils. Stories of Ofsted inspectors grilling headteachers for the reasons why the proportion of four disadvantaged pupils reaching a particular level was below national average were rife. Worse still, this inquisition extended to pupils with SEND. Treated as a group and often small in number, their results were compared to various averages, and teachers would have to explain the existence of the attainment gap.

Whilst Ofsted has taken positive steps by removing much of the focus on attainment gaps in the IDSR, such conversations still take place within multi-academy trusts, and with local authorities and school improvement consultants. It must be challenged and resisted if we are to win the battle against data nonsense.

 Dataproof Your School

The other form of gap analysis is that provided by standardised tests. Unless the tests are online or the test provider offers a marking service, this is usually a laborious process involving the entering of a series of 1s and 0s – denoting correct and incorrect answers – onto a spreadsheet or online system. If pupils take three papers – which is common – and there are 30 pupils in the class, then this can add up to thousands of scores requiring entry onto the system each term.

The scores are then summarised, and results are compared to those of the reference sample, which gives an idea of how well the class are doing in a national context. Output will show, for example, the percentage of questions the class answered correctly in a particular domain of mathematics alongside the sample average for comparison. This may be useful at class level but is less so for pupils with SEND who have specific barriers to learning and for whom any comparison to an average is therefore meaningless. Beyond the marking of the test and scrutiny of the pupil's answers, there is little value in attempting to carry out any further analysis involving national data unless it is drawn from a specially selected sample of contextually similar children. Even then, it is probably not worth the effort.

In short, when it comes to pupils with SEND, there are no groups or averages or benchmarks to compare against; there are only individuals. And that's where engagement and provision mapping come in.

6.2.3.4 Engagement

In July 2020, the Department for Education published details of the Engagement Model, which will replace the remaining system of P Scales used to assess pupils that are not engaged in subject-specific study. It replaces an absolute model of attainment with a relative one and, as such, moves assessment of pupils with profound and multiple learning difficulties away from a criteria-linked, hierarchical, numerical scale to a relative, pupil-centred approach. It was felt that P Scales were no longer fit for purpose and had come to be seen as a progression model, with similar issues to the old system of national curriculum levels. As many pupils did not and cannot be expected to progress systematically through P Scales in a linear fashion, a model whereby pupils are assessed in terms of their engagement relative to their specific targets is deemed to be more appropriate. One of the main principles of the report is that 'engagement identifies and celebrates all pupils' progress, including linear and lateral progress, the consolidation and maintenance of knowledge, skills and concepts and the prevention or slowing of a decline in pupils' performance' (Standards and Testing Agency, 2020: 5). This is an important point as it challenges the traditional view of progress. All targets are challenging regardless of academic 'level' and pupils can display higher or lower degrees of engagement – and therefore make good progress – in pursuit of these.

There are five areas of engagement covered by the model:

- Exploration
- Realisation
- Anticipation
- Persistence
- Initiation.

Schools will monitor a child's engagement in each of these areas against the targets set in their individual learning plans. Importantly, the model does not prescribe a particular format for the data that schools should collect, and there is no requirement for any data to be submitted to the government. This means schools are free to come up with their own methods of assessment, recording and analysis.

As stated, the engagement model is intended to apply only to those pupils who are not engaged in subject-specific study. These will be pupils with profound and often multiple special educational needs. However, such an approach has wider appeal. In addition to collecting data on attainment – teacher assessments, standardised scores, reading ages and the like – schools should also consider monitoring engagement in key developmental areas, which can be cross-referenced with academic data. Engagement could simply be recorded as low, medium or high, or as a number on a five-point scale, and would be similar to the effort/attitude to learning grades commonly collected in secondary schools.

Data of this type is the missing link in many school's assessment systems in that it bridges the gap between contextual information and academic results.

6.2.3.5 Provision mapping

The SEND Code of Practice (DfE, 2015: 105) states that:

> Provision maps are an efficient way of showing all the provision that the school makes which is additional to and different from that which is offered through the school's curriculum. The use of provision maps can help SENCOs to maintain an overview of the programmes and interventions used with different groups of pupils and provide a basis for monitoring the levels of intervention.

A provision map should collate all relevant data relating to pupils with SEND, to monitor their progress over time, evaluate the effectiveness of additional support, and report key information to parents. And this is where a good assessment database comes into its own.

Full name	Term of Birth	SEND Provision	Pupil Premium	YR Sum EYFS GLD EYFSP	Y1 Sum Reading Phonics Score	Y2 Sum Reading SAT TA	2020/21 Spr Persistence Engagement	2020/21 Aut Reading Age	2020/21 Spr Reading Age	Reading progress from 2020/21 Aut to 2020/21 Spr Age
Pupil-005	Autumn	EHC Plan	N	Not GLD	40	WTS	High	9y 1m [-13m]	9y 8m [-10m]	7m
Pupil-006	Summer	SEN Support	N	GLD	36	EXS	High	8y 1m [-17m]	9y 4m [-5m]	15m
Pupil-008	Summer	SEN Support	N	Not GLD	20	EXS	Medium	6y 5m [-13m]	7y 2m [-7m]	9m
Pupil-009	Autumn	SEN Support	N	Not GLD	40	WTS	Medium	7y 5m [-8m]	8y 2m [-2m]	9m
Pupil-010	Spring	SEN Support	N	GLD	40	WTS	Low	8y 9m [0m]	9y 2m [+1m]	5m
Pupil-011	Autumn	SEN Support	N	Not GLD	32	WTS	High	6y 9m [-15m]	7y 9m [-6m]	12m
Pupil-012	Autumn	EHC Plan	N	Not GLD	32	EXS	Medium	5y 9m [-26m]	6y 8m [-19m]	11m
Summary				Not GLD	34	WTS	Medium	8y 2m	9y 1m	10m
Reading Club — 10 pupils — 83%										
Pupil-001	Autumn	SEN Support	N	Not GLD	40	WTS	Medium	10y 2m [-10m]	11y 1m [-2m]	11m
Pupil-002	Spring	SEN Support	N	Not GLD	40	WTS	Medium	9y 3m [-17m]	10y 1m [-10m]	10m
Pupil-003	Spring	SEN Support	N	Not GLD	32	WTS	Medium	8y 9m [-13m]	10y 9m [+8m]	24m
Pupil-004	Spring	SEN Support	N	GLD	20	EXS	Low	9y 7m [-1m]	9y 9m [-3m]	2m
Pupil-005	Autumn	EHC Plan	N	Not GLD	40	WTS	High	9y 1m [-13m]	9y 8m [-10m]	7m
Pupil-008	Summer	SEN Support	N	Not GLD	20	EXS	Medium	6y 5m [-13m]	7y 2m [-7m]	9m
Pupil-009	Autumn	SEN Support	N	Not GLD	40	WTS	Medium	7y 5m [-8m]	8y 2m [-2m]	9m
Pupil-010	Spring	SEN Support	N	GLD	40	WTS	Low	8y 9m [0m]	9y 2m [+1m]	5m
Pupil-011	Autumn	SEN Support	N	Not GLD	32	WTS	High	6y 9m [-15m]	7y 9m [-6m]	12m

Figure 6.1. Section of a simple provision map showing contextual information, some prior attainment history, level of engagement, and change in reading age between the autumn and spring terms. Pupils (fictional) are grouped by support strategy, for which a summary row is provided.

Source: Insight.

Pupils will have specific targets linked to their individual learning plans and will have additional support put in place to help them achieve those targets, which may be social and developmental as well as academic. The first stage in developing a provision map is to record these targets in a system – including the dates they are set and reviewed – alongside important contextual information, assessment data, commentary, and a list of the types of provision that have been implemented to support the child. Ideally, the school's assessment database will include a bank of the types of provision offered that can easily be assigned to pupils with SEND to build up a record of the support they are receiving. It is useful if the provision bank includes associated costs for each item – hourly rates, subscription fees, one-off purchase price for resources – to enable analysis of cost effectiveness.

The assessment database should then allow teachers to collate each pupil's record of provision into a table alongside their targets, contextual details and assessment history to build that all-important picture over time. The provision map is therefore a comprehensive document of support and achievement; it is indispensable for monitoring and reviewing practice, reporting to key audiences, and ensuring that the school meets the guidelines set out in the SEND code of practice (DfE, 2015).

A good assessment database will be able to build a bespoke provision map quickly and efficiently. It should also be capable of grouping and summarising the data in various ways – by provision type, SEND category or class, for example. Whilst group averages are to be treated with extreme caution, viewing summary data for each type of provision – for example, the average change in reading age – may reveal something about their effectiveness, or at least prompt further inquiry.

Box 6.2 — A structured approach to provision mapping

Provision mapping is an ongoing process used strategically to plan, monitor and evaluate provision for pupils with additional needs, including those with SEND. Provision mapping supports the development and recording of interventions to match the assessed needs of pupils across a school and enables leaders to evaluate the impact of the provision on pupil progress.

The provision mapping process involves analysis and use of a range of data types to support leaders to make decisions at both a strategic and individual pupil level. When undertaking provision mapping, it can be helpful for schools to consider the use of data throughout the following six-step process or cycle:

Step 1: Audit need to identify pupils

The cycle starts with a review of the SEN Register to consider the range of provision required across the broad areas of need and to identify individual pupils who would benefit from this additional provision.

Step 2: Review what works

Leaders will need to consider evaluations of any current provision they have in place, identifying what works well and what doesn't work. Where there are gaps in provision it may be helpful to review some of the available research into the effectiveness of interventions, e.g. from the Education Endowment Foundation.

Step 3: Identify suitable resources

This step involves identifying the available budget and staffing resource. Auditing the skills, knowledge and confidence of staff via an audit can support leaders to identify any professional development required to ensure provision is delivered effectively.

Step 4: Develop high-quality provision and map

Once pupils have been identified, provision agreed and resources secured, this information can be recorded on a provision map. The provision map is the tool that holds all the relevant data and is likely to include:

- Basic data for each pupil (name, date and term of birth, year group, class)
- Attendance and year pupil joined the school
- Pupil SEND information (SEN support/EHCP, area(s) of need)
- Level of engagement and effort grades
- List of additional provision types/names with associated costs
- Provision details (length, frequency, group size, staff involved, costs)
- Targets for individual pupils/provisions

(Continued)

- Assessment data for individual pupils
- Baseline and exit data (see step 5)

Step 5: Ensure robust assessment and tracking

Baseline and exit data will need to be established for any intervention in order to measure impact on individual pupil progress. The nature of this data will depend on the type of provision, but can include both quantitative and qualitative information such as:

- Results of national assessments (in England this includes Early Years Foundation Stage Profile, Phonics, Key Stage 1 and Key Stage 2)
- Teacher assessments including indication of curriculum year the pupil is working within
- Results of standardised assessment in reading, spelling and maths including scores and ages
- Changes in scores and assessment age over time
- Social, emotional and mental health questionnaires
- Pupil and parent feedback
- Teacher/Teaching Assistant feedback
- Observational data

Step 6: Monitor and evaluate impact

The above information based on individual pupil progress can then be collated and analysed in order to evaluate the overall effectiveness of each additional provision. This will support strategic decision making for the next cycle of provision mapping.

The six-step process outlined above provides a suggested model for schools. However, there is no 'one-size-fits-all' approach to provision mapping and schools should continually review and refine their process to find what works for them.

Natalie Packer, SEND Consultant

The most important aspect of provision mapping is its focus on individuals rather than on groups of pupils. Presenting each child's specific needs, provision, context and progress in this way will help dispel the myth of a group bound by a single characteristic, whose progress is linear and comparable. Instead, we see them as individuals with often complex needs, whose journeys do not fit a neat model and whose progress is difficult to define and impossible to measure.

6.3 Assessment and support for pupils working well above curriculum expectations

In the years from 2015 to 2019, around one in five pupils taking GCSEs attained a grade 7 or above (FFT, 2019). At Key Stage 2, 27% of pupils reached the higher standard in Reading and Maths, 36% reached the higher standard in Grammar, Punctuation and Spelling and 20% of pupils were assessed as reaching the higher standard in writing (DfE, 2019).

Assessing pupils who are working at higher levels than their peers presents various issues. The first is that any written assessment has a ceiling effect, in that there is a hard limit for those who achieve full marks on any paper. An adaptive assessment, which presents pupils with test items based on earlier answers during the assessment, can mitigate against this issue; even so, those working at the highest end of the spectrum will encounter a ceiling beyond which they cannot progress.

In addition, written assessments cannot include too many test items which differentiate between those at the highest end of the spectrum as these items will not provide useful information about those working within the typical range and may have unintended side-effects which reduce the validity of inferences made as a result of test outcomes.

We do need to identify pupils working well above expectations, however, and to build a picture of the educational history of those outliers at the higher end of the spectrum. Once these pupils have been identified, we need to decide how they might be supported.

6.3.1 Assessing pupils working well above expectations

A dataproof school will use regular assessments to build a picture over time of pupils' academic attainment (see Chapters 1, 8 and 9 for further details). This will identify pupils who are working well above expectations compared to their peers, both within their classes and cohorts, and against the national picture. As we see above, we would expect around 20% of pupils nationally to be in this group; individual schools or groups of schools will build a picture of the broad percentage of pupils in their classes and cohorts. In any given subject, this is likely to be somewhere near 6 pupils in a class of 30, although the variation between cohorts will naturally be quite wide.

Annual standardised assessments will identify this group, but schools may wish to consider whether they need further assessments to support their decision making. There are very few commercial assessments that are available, as this group tends not to attract as much attention as the group working below national expectations.

You might want to consider using Cognitive Ability Tests (CATs), which can reveal areas of strength and weakness which underlie pupils' academic ability. Whilst these are more common at secondary level, they are available for younger pupils and may provide useful information on which you might wish to act.

6.3.2 Supporting primary pupils working well above expectations

In English primary schools, pupils are often – although not always – placed in within-class groups based on an attainment measure of recent academic performance. Research evidence suggests that this is generally beneficial for pupils working well above expectations – although lower attaining pupils do not benefit as much (Education Endowment Foundation (EEF), 2018b).

Using attainment measures of academic performance to group pupils is, as discussed in Chapter 3, complicated, as assessment is often extremely noisy. As always, using data over time should help to ensure pupils are grouped more accurately. A further issue is that there are many underlying factors which might make identifying pupils working well above expectations more complicated: age within cohort is, for example, an important underlying factor in most assessment in primary schools. As a result, younger pupils who are working well above expectations may not be immediately recognised as such. Likewise, there may be other contextual factors which may need to be considered.

With these caveats in mind, what should primary schools do to support pupils who are working well above expectations? Research into the effectiveness of initiatives such as the Young Gifted and Talented programme, which the UK government ran from 2002 to 2010, is limited, particularly for children under eleven. Organisations such as Potential Plus (a charity founded in 1967 as the National Association for Gifted Children) suggest a focus on planning for challenge in and beyond the classroom, and the social and emotional development of pupils working well above expectations.

In truth, there is very little evidence to suggest that there are effective ways to support primary age children at the upper end of the ability spectrum, beyond those which underpin effective schooling which we discussed in Chapter 1.

With this in mind, as a dataproof primary school you should:

- Ensure that you build a picture over time of those pupils working well above expectations
- Adapt the curriculum for each class/cohort as appropriate for your context
- Ensure that contextual factors are considered when grouping/considering curriculum for classes and cohorts.

6.3.3 Supporting secondary pupils working well above expectations

In English secondary schools, pupils are frequently grouped into sets or streams as they progress through school (EEF, 2018a). Setting involves placing pupils in a given year group into specific classes – usually based on prior assessments – for particular subjects (such as mathematics or English). Streaming involves placing pupils into classes for all or most of their lessons.

In our experience, pupils in secondaries tend to start school in mixed ability groups for most subjects; mathematics sets tend to be introduced early in Key Stage 3; by the end of Key Stage 3 most pupils are taught in sets across the curriculum. By Key Stage 4, most schools have effectively streamed pupils based on their choices at the end of Key Stage 3, and there are likely to be within-stream sets for science subjects within Key Stage 4.

As the EEF notes, 'The evidence suggests that setting and streaming has a very small negative impact for low and mid-range attaining learners, and a very small positive impact for higher attaining pupils'. This suggests that a dataproof school should keep pupils in mixed ability classes where possible as this has the greatest benefit for the school as a whole. As pupils progress through secondary education, however, those working well above expectations for their age group are increasingly likely to be grouped together.

Much of the support for academically able pupils provided at a national level has focused on opening up pathways into higher education. This is based on research suggesting that disadvantaged pupils are systematically excluded from higher education pathways from a relatively early age. In essence, if you are not aware of the options open to you at 18 and do not study the right subjects from Key Stage 4 onwards, you are less likely to be in a position to access courses at the more exclusive universities.

To tackle this issue, the Young Gifted and Talented programme of 2002–2010 aimed to provide additional support for the top 5% of 11- to 19-year-olds, with a programme of summer schools and outreach activities (House of Commons Library, 2020). Since 2010, this work has largely been undertaken by the Sutton Trust, a leading UK charity which aims to enable disadvantaged pupils to access elite universities. Other organisations such as The Brilliant Club also work in this area.

As one metric that secondary schools are judged on is outcomes for pupils, there is a clear incentive to ensure that those pupils who may benefit from a place at an elite university are given the best possible support to achieve that aim. Beyond this aim, schools should also look to put in place context-specific support for those working well above expectations, and this support should begin as soon as is appropriate for your context.

This may be a programme of awareness-raising events and opportunities (such as pathway talks, visiting speakers and visits to external institutions), curriculum opportunities (options to study one-year GCSEs in Year 10 with dedicated study time allocated in Year 11, for example) or involvement with national programmes to support those at the upper end of the ability spectrum.

With this in mind, as a dataproof secondary school you should:

- Ensure that you build a picture over time of those pupils working well above expectations
- Develop a programme of awareness-raising events
- Plan curriculum streams which maximise opportunities for pupils working well above national expectations
- Partner with external organisations as appropriate
- Ensure that contextual factors are considered when setting/considering curriculum for classes and cohorts.

6.4 Summary

For the sake of convenience, it is tempting to apply a blanket approach, to shoehorn pupils onto a one-size-fits-all flightpath that assumes they all progress through the curriculum at the same rate. Alternatively, we could go to the other extreme and fall into the trap of believing that the more subdivisions we have, the more progress it proves, and end up with a complicated, asymmetrical assessment scheme with numerous categories dedicated to documenting each of the 'small steps' that certain groups of pupils make. These are not useful approaches; these are approaches designed to meet someone else's demands and they should be resisted. Schools also need to recognise that checking off long lists of learning objectives is probably not telling teachers anything they didn't already know and that getting pupils to sit tests intended for younger or older children may not be providing useful information either. More suitable and diagnostic methods of assessment are available.

For some pupils we need more data and for some we need less; and what works for the majority will not work for all. Teachers obviously tailor their practice to cater for the needs of individual pupils, and the dataproof school recognises that the data they record should be similarly individualised. When it comes to the outliers – those pupils that sit in the narrow tails of the bell curve – schools need more regular and detailed information to monitor their learning and evaluate the effectiveness of additional support. This is especially the case for those working well below curriculum expectations.

Pupils with high needs do not form a homogenous group – there is no real value in averages and there are no suitable national benchmarks to compare them to. The most powerful data tool is a table that builds a picture of provision and assessment over time. The dataproof school will block out the noise calling for measures of 'small steps of progress' and understands that, ultimately, it's about narrative not numbers.

References

Christodoulou, D. (2016) *Making Good Progress?* Oxford: Oxford University Press (pp. 79–111).

Department for Education (DfE) (2015) *Special Educational Needs and Disability Code of Practice: 0 to 25 Years* [Online]. Available at: https://assets.publishing.service.gov.uk/government/uploads/system/uploads/attachment_data/file/398815/SEND_Code_of_Practice_January_2015.pdf (Accessed 7 May 2021) (p. 105).

Department for Education (DfE) (2017) *Performance – P Scale – Attainment Targets for Pupils with Special Educational Needs* [Online]. Available at: https://assets.publishing.service.gov.uk/government/uploads/system/uploads/attachment_data/file/903590/Performance_-_P_Scale_-_attainment_targets_for_pupils_with_special_educational_needs_June_2017.pdf (Accessed 6 May 2021).

Department for Education (DfE) (2019) *National Curriculum Assessments at Key Stage 2 in England, 2019.* Available at: https://assets.publishing.service.gov.uk/government/uploads/system/uploads/attachment_data/file/830285/KS2_Provisional_publication_text_2019.pdf. (Accessed 8 May 2021).

Department for Education (DfE) (2021) *Complete the School Census* [Online]. Available at: www.gov.uk/guidance/complete-the-school-census/find-a-school-census-code (accessed 6 May 2021).

Education Endowment Foundation (EEF) (2018a) *Within-class Attainment Grouping.* Available at: https://educationendowmentfoundation.org.uk/pdf/toolkit/?id=2618&t=Teaching%20and%20Learning%20Toolkit&e=2618&s=. (Accessed 8 May 2021).

Education Endowment Foundation (EEF) (2018b) *Setting or Streaming.* Available at: https://educationendowmentfoundation.org.uk/pdf/toolkit/?id=127&t=Teaching%20and%20Learning%20Toolkit&e=127&s=. (Accessed 8 May 2021).

Fischer Family Trust (FFT) (2019) GCSE results 2019: The main trends in grades and entries. Available at: https://ffteducationdatalab.org.uk/2019/08/gcse-results-2019-the-main-trends-in-grades-and-entries/#:~:text=Overall%20grades%20have%20gone%20up,-compared%20to%2066.6%25%20last%20year. (Accessed 8 May 2021).

House of Commons Library (2020) 'Support for more able and talented children in schools (UK)'. Available at: https://researchbriefings.files.parliament.uk/documents/CBP-9065/CBP-9065.pdf. (Accessed 8 May 2021).

Ofsted (2021) *The School Inspection Handbook* (para. 354) [Online]. Available at: www.gov.uk/government/publications/school-inspection-handbook-eif/school-inspection-handbook (Accessed 7 May 2021).

Rochford Review (2016) *The Rochford Review: Final Report* [Online]. Available at: https://assets.publishing.service.gov.uk/government/uploads/system/uploads/attachment_data/file/561411/Rochford_Review_Report_v5_PFDA.pdf (Accessed 6 May 2021).

Spielman, A. (2018) Amanda Spielman at the Bryanston Education Summit [Online]. Available at: www.gov.uk/government/speeches/amanda-spielman-at-the-bryanston-education-summit (Accessed 5 May 2021).

Standards and Testing Agency (2020) *The Engagement Model* [Online]. Available at: https://assets.publishing.service.gov.uk/government/uploads/system/uploads/attachment_data/file/903458/Engagement_Model_Guidance_2020.pdf (Accessed 4 November 2021).

TRACKING SYSTEMS

7.1   Where did 'tracking' go wrong?

Once upon a time, when national curriculum levels still existed in England, Ofsted, the schools' inspectorate, were heavily reliant on a school's assessment data to inform the inspection process. Not just the results of statutory assessments – they still pay close attention to those – but the outcomes of regular checks on pupils' learning. For many years, schools operated in a strange, twilight world where non-standardised and unvalidated data could, potentially, sway an inspection. This came to be known as 'tracking data', and complex systems were invented to store, crunch and present it in appealing and seemingly irrefutable graphs and charts. Tracking systems – that started life as spreadsheets – soon became big business: software sold on a promise of its Ofsted-boosting powers. A tool elevated to the status of oracle. A huge industry boomed around generating numbers for Ofsted, and other agencies, that acted as proxies for pupils' learning and supposedly 'proved' the progress they made. Numbers that kept the wolf from the door. And there were two rules: the numbers always went up, usually by a mythical point per term, and no one *ever* questioned the meaning of the numbers. The system required total buy-in from all stakeholders for the illusion to be maintained. An uneasy silence reigned for well over a decade. No one broke the omerta of tracking.

The removal of national curriculum levels in 2014 was intended to provoke debate and initiate a seismic shift in approach to assessment, but most schools, despite advice to the contrary, continued with existing systems that simply rebadged levels:

> tracking software, which has been used widely as a tool for measuring progress with levels, cannot, and should not, be adapted to assess understanding of a curriculum that recognises depth and breadth of understanding as

of equal value to linear progression. (Commission on Assessment without Levels, 2015)

Here was a clear declaration that progress was a complicated, multi-faceted concept that could not be measured in simple, linear terms. Attempts to do so would require wilful disregard of the reality of learning. But still schools persisted with simplistic, levels-style progress measures because that was what they believed Ofsted expected to see. Furthermore, it was how tracking systems were built: the assumption of linear progression through content was hardwired and central to their purpose. No, it didn't really align with the new curriculum with focus on mastery but no matter – the numbers trumped everything. But then things began to change.

As discussed in Chapter 2, between 2015 and 2019, Ofsted went from a position of requiring internal tracking data in a particular format (i.e. levels), to ostensibly working with any kind of assessment data (but still preferring neat, points-based, quasi-levels measures, let's be honest), to no longer requiring any tracking data, and it wouldn't be long before they turned their back on it altogether. Ofsted would even start to challenge schools on the volume and purpose of the data they collect.

The final nail was hammered home in 2019 when the inspectorate took the decision to no longer take a school's internal assessment data into consideration during an inspection. The Chief Inspector announced that conversations about pupils' learning were more constructive than 'byzantine number systems' (Spielman, 2018). After years of taking internal data into consideration, they had realised that much of it is non-standardised, unvalidated, and could even be completely made up.

Of course, this could be interpreted to mean that assessment data is obsolete, and that speaks volumes about the way data is perceived in some schools: as a servant of accountability rather than teaching. A way to keep the wolf from the door. But data is useful. It helps teachers identify potential issues to better support pupils; it allows senior leaders to make informed decisions; and it provides governors with the information they need to ask challenging questions. Ditching data as a result of Ofsted's decision to ignore it is missing the point.

Freed from having to produce data for Ofsted, schools finally have licence to fulfil the promise of assessment without levels and design an approach that is clear, meaningful and fit for purpose. Undeterred, many schools continued in their pursuit of numerical proxies of pupils' progress despite the fact they had no real impact on learning and no one from outside of the school – well, not Ofsted anyway – would look at them. Teachers would even admit, when pressed, that the systems they spent so much time feeding were not providing any actionable information. But change was in the air and more and more were starting to ask questions about the validity and purpose of the data they spent so much time gathering.

When you stop to think about it, measuring progress was like measuring the length of happiness.

But that is what schools have been trying to do, seemingly forever. Everyone was fixated on measuring the immeasurable and the systems schools employed had bet the farm on it. They were barking up the wrong tree.

7.2   What are tracking systems for?

First, we should address the elephant in the room: the name. The phrase 'tracking system' is inherently problematic for two reasons: 1) 'tracking' implies measuring something over time – in this case, learning – which probably cannot be measured; and 2) 'tracking' also has somewhat sinister connotations. What – or who – are we tracking? Pupils? Or the teachers themselves? Certainly, in many schools, systems used ostensibly to measure pupil progress are eyed with suspicion by the teachers who might spend hours entering data only to get nothing of value in return. In some cases, teachers may submit data to the office or to a senior leader via a spreadsheet, or even on paper, that is then to be inputted onto 'The System'. They do not see the output and there is no tangible benefit in terms of their practice. It is a data black hole. Such scenarios are not conducive to data integrity and therefore risk creating a negative data culture in schools, which helps no one.

Instead, we need our system to provide a 'warts and all' picture of learning and that requires a culture shift. Data that is collected needs to be 1) accurate, 2) proportionate and 3) useful. There is a fine balance between impact on learning and impact on workload and it is all too easy to tip the scales the wrong way. The *Making Data Work* report recommends that 'Ofsted inspectors should ask questions about whether schools' attainment data collections are proportionate, represent an efficient use of school resources, and are sustainable for staff' (Teacher Workload Advisory Group, 2018). We must recognise that the more onerous the process becomes the less reliable our data will be. Is the answer to measure more, more often? Or is it to have the right amount of the right sort of information? Sometimes the processes we put in place to improve things can have the opposite effect.

Let's press the reset button and start again. From now on we should refer to our systems as *assessment databases*. These will not be used to measure the immeasurable or monitor teacher performance. Neither will they be viewed as assessment *systems* because they do not assess. Instead, they will act as libraries of useful information and will be built from the classroom upwards to help keep teachers informed about the pupils' progress.

Systems need be easy to set up, maintain and use. They should be customisable so schools can store all their data in one place in whatever format they choose without having to make compromises to fit the rules of the system. They should make reporting to governors and parents a straightforward process, and – perhaps a factor that is often overlooked – they should be engaging. A well-designed system will be well used, and this has two key benefits: data is more likely to be timely and accurate, and teachers will be better informed.

Any summary data that is generated for senior leaders, governors, trust boards, school improvement advisors and other external agencies will be a by-product of a system that is primarily designed to support children's learning. There will be no abstract numbers, all the data will have purpose and meaning, it will make lives easier by reducing workload, and teachers should have equal access to all data contained in the system. Locking teachers out of parts, or all, of the system – unless required due to the sensitive nature of its contents – will only increase suspicion about the purpose of data and potentially erode its integrity.

Perhaps most important of all is ensuring that the assessment database aligns with the school's curriculum, assessment policy and wider data strategy. Only then can we be certain that it will fulfil its intended purpose. To dataproof your school, it is therefore recommended that you wait until everything else is in place before implementing your system to avoid it influencing any part of the process.

7.3   What are the benefits of an assessment database?

An assessment database will ensure that your data is:

- Secure
- Accessible
- Analysable.

As a result, teachers will be able to retrieve information quickly, and preparing and presenting data to key audiences such as governors will be a straightforward task. Whilst a spreadsheet can perform these functions, data management is likely to become a more centralised and specialist job, with reliance on a single member of staff who has the skills and time to dedicate to development and administration of the system. Schools that are fortunate to have a dedicated data manager may go down the route of building a series of integrated, bespoke systems, but even those schools need to ensure they have future-proofed themselves against the risks posed by that key person leaving their post.

It is therefore little wonder that many schools have purchased commercial systems, and these should provide a useful, simple and manageable solution to a school's data needs. There are, however, some important things to consider before buying a system:

- **Customisation:** it is vital that systems can be adapted to meet the needs of the school – rather than the school compromising to fit the system – and can be modified as and when processes develop and change.
- **Any data in any format:** the system must be capable of storing all the school's data in whatever format they want it stored in. Do not accept a system that is out of alignment with the school's assessment policy.
- **Quick analysis:** it is all very well having all your data in one place, but the system needs to be able to quickly analyse and present it. Having to resort to spreadsheets and calculators may be a sign you need to rethink your system.
- **Links to MIS:** a live link to the school's Management Information System (MIS) means that pupil information is always up to date.
- **Access for all:** universal rather than centralised access to pupil information will result in better informed teaching staff and foster a more positive data culture across the school.
- **Online:** whilst not essential, online systems are undeniably useful. Cloud storage is secure, abundant, and cheap or even free, and means that data can be accessed from home as well as in school. Stringent data security is imperative, but having access to data online makes life easier. This was particularly pertinent during the lockdowns of 2020–21.

The main purpose of a school's assessment database is, therefore, to store all assessment data in one place, to provide teachers and senior leaders with quick and easy access to that data, to help them analyse it accurately and efficiently, and to facilitate the presentation and reporting of data to key audiences, including governors and parents.

7.4   What data should an assessment database contain?

The database stores each pupil's assessment history alongside useful contextual information so teachers can quickly gain a detailed insight into a child's journey through school. To do this job well, the system needs to be capable of storing any data in any format for all the pupils in the school. The aim is to construct a detailed picture of learning over time, and to do this our database might contain:

- Contextual information
- Results of statutory national tests and assessments
- Scores from standardised tests

- Teacher judgements
- Baseline scores
- Reading scheme level/book band
- Phonics phase
- Comparative judgement scores
- Reading/spelling/numeracy age
- Targets and predictions
- Effort and attitude to learning grades
- Teachers' comments
- Provisions and interventions
- SEND-specific assessment data
- Extracurricular activities.

The following sections will go through these factors in more detail.

7.4.1 Contextual information

School systems contain a wealth of contextual information that is of huge value to teachers. Such information can provide answers to questions about pupil behaviour and academic performance as well as help anticipate and avoid potential issues.

7.4.1.1 Mobility

Changing school can have an adverse impact on attainment, especially if moves are frequent. How many times have pupils moved school and when did they join the current school? What are the reasons for mobility and how might achievement be affected? The facility to group pupils by the year they joined the school and separate performance data into these groups is a very useful feature of assessment data.

7.4.1.2 Attendance

If children are not in school, they are probably not learning what we want them to. Are there any significant periods of absence? What were the reasons for these? Setting attendance thresholds and grouping pupils by these is a useful function that an assessment database should be able to perform.

7.4.1.3 Month/term of birth

Age in year can have a significant impact on attainment. Gaps between the youngest and oldest pupils in a cohort narrow over time but it is still worth knowing who the youngest in the class are. Are these the pupils that need more support? The assessment database can quickly reveal this by grouping assessment data by term of birth, which will show if it is mostly summer-born pupils that are struggling. Age-standardised scores, provided by many tests, are useful for mitigating age-related issues and these can also be stored in the assessment database.

7.4.1.4 Special educational needs

An obvious one, but who are the pupils with SEND, what are their specific needs and how have these changed over time? Are there year groups and classes with higher proportions of SEND than others? How might this affect future results? What additional support have pupils received and how successful was it? The assessment database can store SEND status, area and need, and a list of targeted support, alongside results of diagnostic assessments, such as standardised scores and reading age, as well as commentary. This will enable provision maps to be constructed, which will help track the effectiveness of the provision that has been put in place to support pupils with SEND. An example could be monitoring the change in reading age over time for pupils on a particular intervention. The issues relating to data for pupils with SEND is dealt with in more detail in Chapter 6.

7.4.1.5 English as an additional language (EAL)

Again, this seems obvious, but how much is known about the varying needs of EAL pupils, the support they have received and how effective that support has been? Again, the assessment database can store the results of diagnostic assessments such as scores and ages, alongside other information like EAL proficiency stages and notes. As above, monitoring the change in assessment – for example, phonics scores or reading ages – over time is a useful function of an assessment database.

7.4.1.6 Disadvantaged pupils

Which pupils are eligible for Free School Meals or have been in the last six years? Are there any looked-after children in the cohort? Whilst not definitive, deprivation can be an indicator of lower achievement and having access to this information is important for teachers. The database can store this alongside assessment data and information on any support that has been put in place for these pupils. This will help answer questions about the effectiveness of any such support intended to close gaps between the most disadvantaged pupils and others, which are likely to arise when focusing on the use of the Pupil Premium.

7.4.1.7 Another warning about group-level data

Comparing the results of groups of pupils will always reveal attainment gaps. We could take any defining characteristic – those that wear grey or black socks for example – and there will be a difference in the average scores of those groups. This can lead to kneejerk reactions if we suddenly decide, on the basis of limited data analysis, that underachievement in maths relates predominantly to pupils born in the spring term. We could react by ploughing resources in to meet the apparent needs of this group of pupils, but these things are never so simple in reality. First, there is group size: one pupil in a small group – and in many schools these groups will be small – will have a big effect on results and will skew them. Second, there is the overlap between groups: pupils will fall into any number of groups so it could be, in our example above, that pupils with SEND just happen to be disproportionately represented in the 'spring-born' group in one cohort. Knowledge of overlap between groups is vital and an assessment database should be capable of helping with this. Third, even if there was a particular issue with a group of pupils, it is unlikely to be a trend; it is more likely to be cohort specific. Directing resources to target that group in other cohorts is highly likely to be misplaced.

Some may question whether access to demographic information is helpful or whether it increases assessment bias, and that is a conversation schools need to have. However, analysis shows that certain contextual factors, such as those outlined above, are strong indicators of underperformance and it is therefore most likely beneficial if teachers are aware of them.

One way in which schools are likely to want to group data – and that is more valid than grouping by contextual factors – is by class. Examples are provided in section 7.5 below.

7.4.2 Prior attainment history

It is surprising how many teachers are unaware of pupils' prior attainment and do not know where to find it, but knowledge of the results of national tests is an important part of the jigsaw. To build a picture over time, teachers should know how pupils performed in statutory assessments and at the various key stages. The following is a rundown of the statutory assessments administered in schools in England.

7.4.2.1 Early Years Foundation Stage Profile (EYFSP)

Did all pupils reach a good level of development at the end of the reception year? If not, where were the gaps? Some pupils may have been emerging in one or two early learning goals whilst others may have been emerging in all of them. Did they narrowly miss them at the end of reception and meet them early in Year 1, or were they significantly below for their age? And, of course, some pupils may have exceeded some or all early learning goals. Does Early Years development correlate mainly with month of birth or are other factors at play? The assessment database can keep a record of a pupil's progress towards early learning goals as well as the results of baseline assessments. This record does not have to involve a complicated hierarchical ladder of age bands; a simple 'below/expected/above'-style judgement each term will suffice.

7.4.2.2 Phonics

Did all pupils pass the phonics check? Did they pass it in Year 1 or 2 or not at all? If they did not meet the standard, was it due to a special educational need, a language barrier, or something else? Did they struggle on the real or the 'alien' words? The assessment database can store the result of the statutory assessment as well as the scores from any practice attempts.

7.4.2.3 Key Stage 1

Did pupils meet expected standards in all subjects, or miss it in one, two or all? Were any pupils working below the key stage standards and assessed as pre-key stage? Who achieved greater depth? What were the scaled scores in the reading and maths tests? Were there any discrepancies between the test score and teacher assessment? For example, pupils that achieved a score of 100 or more on the test but received a final assessment of 'working towards expected standards'; or scored below 100 yet met the expected standard. What were the reasons for these discrepancies? Is there any Question Level Analysis (QLA) of Key Stage 1 tests that may point to areas of weakness? Of those pupils that fell short of expected standards, which ones may or may not catch up by the end of Key Stage 2?

7.4.2.4 Key Stage 2

Did all pupils sit tests? If not, why not? Were any assessed as pre-key stage? Of those pupils that did not meet expected standards, did they fall short in just one subject or all of them? Did pupils narrowly miss the threshold or fall a long way short? Were any pupils granted special consideration? Did any achieve high scores in tests or greater depth in writing? Are there discrepancies between the subjects, especially between writing, which is teacher assessed, and reading, maths and grammar, punctuation and spelling, which are based on tests? Have you accessed

Dataproof Your School

the question-level analysis of the tests for pupils in your class? How do answers compare to national averages at item, pupil and domain level? And perhaps most importantly, how do pupils' Key Stage 2 results – and the results of previous practice tests – compare to their Key Stage 1 results? If you are a secondary teacher, are you familiar with Key Stage 2 results of the pupils in your class and have you compared the results of feeder schools? How do the Key Stage 2 results compare to your own baseline assessment and to national averages? Your assessment database should help answer these questions.

7.4.2.5 GCSEs

Chances are that GCSE results will be well known to sixth-form teachers, but this information should be readily accessible on the assessment database.

7.4.2.6 Other statutory assessments

In future years, primary schools in England will also have the results of the multiplication tables check, which may provide some useful information. We will not, however, have the results from the reception baseline, which the government intends to withhold, but schools can keep their own tally of tasks completed correctly and this could be recorded for future reference.

7.4.3 Internal assessment data

This is the data that Ofsted will not be looking at, but that does not mean it's not important information. It certainly should be, otherwise stop gathering it. We will now look at some examples.

7.4.3.1 Baseline data

When pupils enter a school for the first time, for example in reception and Year 7, teachers will usually make an assessment or administer a test. This data will be of interest to teachers of other year groups and will provide the start point for monitoring pupil progress. Comparing pupils' latest assessment against their baseline in a progress matrix (section 7.5.3) is a simple but effective way of doing this. We could, for example, monitor the change in decile or quintile, or the proportions working below, within or above expectations over time.

7.4.3.2 Teacher assessments

Most teachers record an assessment each term. In a primary school this will be in a range of subjects: the core subjects including reading, writing and maths, and possibly foundation subjects, too. In secondary schools, teachers will most likely make assessments in a single subject. The format of these assessments is dealt with in Chapter 9. Assuming assessments are robust and free from distortion they will be of value to other teachers and can be compared to the results of previous assessments or targets. Again, a progress matrix (section 7.5.3) is a simple solution for comparing results of different points in time.

7.4.3.3 Standardised scores

The results of standardised tests from the likes of NFER, Hodder, GL Assessment and Star Assessment provide teachers with unbiased data that reveal where pupils sit within a large, representative national sample. Monitoring standardised scores over time can therefore show if pupils are falling behind or improving in relation to other pupils nationally and help us understand whether pupils are on track to meet certain grades or standards. For those subjects for which commercial standardised tests are not available, tests can be developed and standardised in house, especially in multi-academy trusts or other groups of schools with large numbers of pupils. Comparative judgement is also an option – the No More Marking system will generate scaled scores and age data for writing, which is difficult to produce by other means.

An assessment database should allow categorisation of scores on the basis of school-defined thresholds, which will enable comparison with other types of data such as the results for statutory assessments and targets. The use of scatter plots is another extremely useful tool that assessment databases should provide. These will show how well correlated one set of scores is with another, which will help establish how accurate a predictor of outcome a school's chosen standardised test is. Scatter plots are also highly effective at revealing anomalies such as those pupils that did well on one test but fell short on another.

7.4.3.4 Percentile rank

You can convert standardised and scaled scores into percentile rank to produce a common currency, which will help improve understanding of data that look similar but are inherently different. Percentile rank has the added benefit of being more widely understood than standardised scores. Monitoring the change in pupils' national percentile rank over time can be a useful way of assessing progress and can be aggregated to group or cohort level for reporting purposes. Where no nationally standardised data is available – that's most subjects beyond English and maths, which is problematic in secondary education – schools can simply monitor the change in each pupil's rank position relative to others in the cohort from entry onwards. This is, of course, a zero-sum game if aggregated but can be useful at individual pupil level. Again, groups of schools can utilise the power of their greater numbers to improve the reliability of percentiles. An assessment database should store these rank scores, show change over time, group pupils into, say, deciles or quintiles, and calculate average rank scores of groups and cohorts where appropriate. A progress matrix (section 7.5.3) could be used to show the shifts of pupils between quintiles.

7.4.3.5 Estimates and targets

In the UK, many schools use FFT, which provides nationally benchmarked outcomes based on pupils' prior attainment. The assessment database should be capable of importing estimates so that all teachers, regardless of year, can view and compare them to the latest and previous assessments. This can help improve understanding of how potential results relate to prior attainment. The assessment database should contain any targets a school sets – if they set them – and easily allow comparison with other assessment data.

7.4.3.6 Age equivalent scores

Many standardised tests, including those aimed at pupils with SEND, provide reading, spelling and even maths ages; and comparative judgement (see Chapter 5) generates writing ages. An assessment database should store this age data, show the difference between a pupil's assessed and chronological age, and calculate the change in assessed age over time. We might be interested in the change in reading age over the course of a three-month period of targeted support, for example. In this case, we could set an 'expected' rate of improvement of three months in terms of reading age and the system would then colour code pupils according to their gain over the period. If we wanted to monitor the effectiveness of specific interventions, the system could calculate the average age equivalent score for the pupils in receipt of each type of support and show how those have changed over time. We may find that pupils' reading ages improve more on some interventions than others, which raises questions about what works well and what does not. As always, however, we must take the noisiness of such data into account and exercise caution before drawing any conclusions.

7.4.3.7 Mock examinations

In most schools, pupils will practise in advance of national tests. The results can be entered onto the assessment database and compared to targets. Using scatter plots to compare the results of mock examinations to actual results can help predict outcomes in future years.

7.4.3.8 Another warning about tracking learning objectives

Many systems, especially those used in primary schools, have a module that allows teachers to record assessments for individual learning objectives. These may be drawn from the school's own curriculum or, as is often the case, they may be end-of-year or key stage statements lifted word for word from the programmes of study of the national curriculum. Either way, the aim is the same: record each pupil's competence in specific areas of each subject. Some systems will automatically generate a 'teacher assessment' from this data, assigning a pupil into a category based on the proportion of objectives checked off the list: a process of assessment by numbers rather than professional judgement.

Following the implementation of the new national curriculum in England there were attempts to minimise the number of these objectives, recognising the workload that recording numerous judgements would entail. But over time, they proliferated as schools sought to tighten up teacher assessment, making it more structured and supposedly less subjective. Unfortunately, multiplying the number of statements by the number of pupils and assessment points results in thousands of records per year and a system that is clearly unsustainable. The old paper-based system of APP (Assessing Pupil Progress), which was intended to guide assessment for small samples of pupils, has been rolled out en masse in digital form in many settings. Teachers are now spending hours ticking off, scoring and RAG rating vast lists of learning objectives.

To what aim? It was done in the belief that it would reveal gaps in pupils' learning. But this is a fallacy: it is highly unlikely this process can tell teachers anything they didn't already know because it is based on what they knew in the first place. It is also unlikely that other teachers will use it to glean information about pupils' prior learning; they are more likely to speak to the relevant teacher directly. Furthermore, the onerous nature of the process often causes teachers to leave the completion of the grids until the last minute and flood fill them, which speaks volumes about their perception of the value of the exercise. This laborious process, which many have come to believe is essential and 'formative', is symptomatic of an 'audit culture' (Teacher Workload Advisory Group, 2018) that exists in many schools. We need to be very honest about the effect such practices have both on learning and on workload.

7.5 Reporting summary data

It is inevitable that schools are going to have to report data to someone somewhere at some point. School improvement partners, governors and boards of trustees are the obvious examples, and for such audiences we require aggregated data presented in reports that summarise a school's performance.

Reporting to governors is a standard function of any assessment database and schools should be able to quickly run reports that present key information to governors including the results of statutory assessments as well as the current picture based on internal data. Ideally, the system will present concise information in a clear and simple 'on-a-page' format without having to resort to exporting to a spreadsheet for further manipulation.

Reporting requirements can be the driving force behind assessment and data collection in many schools and the risk of distortion is clear if the stakes are high. Schools need to ensure that accurate data for teaching is the priority and that numbers are not generated solely for reporting purposes. So, what can we report?

7.5.1 Results of statutory assessments

Results of statutory assessments against national figures over time are essential and a report showing the last three years' results is recommended. In England, this would include the results from the Early Years Foundation Stage Profile, the Phonics Check, Key Stage 1 assessments, the Multiplication Tables Check, tests at Key Stage 2, and GCSE and A Level exams, and any related key performance indicators such as national measures of progress. The Department for Education's Analyse School Performance system provides some useful information but does a poor job of collating it into a simple, summary report. This is where a school's own assessment database comes in. Make sure it presents results in a clear, easy to understand format that will act as a useful reference and enable audiences such as governors to ask informed questions.

7.5.2 Performance of current cohorts

Again, the rule is: keep things simple. Do not stretch your data beyond its elastic limit and attempt to make it do what it is not designed to do. In other words, do not invent stuff to keep other people happy.

7.5.2.1 Primary schools

Report the proportions of pupils working below, towards, within and above expectations at key points in time for the core subjects of reading, writing and maths.

Those points could be the end of foundation stage or Key Stage 1, the end of the previous year and the latest term in the current year; and the assessment may be based on a teacher's judgement or a standardised test, or a combination where the former is informed by the latter. Monitoring percentages working within or above expectations over time will give an idea of how standards are changing across the school, and audiences such as governors should focus on asking questions about the effectiveness of the support provided for those working below expectations, especially those working outside of the age-appropriate curriculum who will often have special educational needs.

7.5.2.2 Secondary schools

Summary data in Key Stage 4 is inevitably going to focus on percentages of pupils on track to achieve specific GCSE grades, and how these compare to previous years' results, targets or estimated outcomes based on pupils' start points. Key Stage 3 is more complicated, but 'working at' or 'working towards' GCSE grades derived from simplistic, linear flightpaths should be avoided, and sub-GCSE grades – for example, Grade 5+ or Grade 6.5 – just give the illusion of accuracy. If internal assessments are to be graded in Key Stage 3, then a non-GCSE-style scale should be used to avoid inference.

Alternatively, adopting a similar approach to primary schools (see above) is worth considering, as is tracking national rank from Key Stage 2. The latter would show whether there is an increasing proportion of pupils in the highest national quintile, for example, but this is only feasible in subjects where standardised tests are available. As previously discussed, groups of schools can use their greater numbers to standardise the results of internal tests, which may provide a better proxy for national rank and allow comparable reporting for other subjects. Systems such as Smartgrade facilitate this process.

A summary of effort, behaviour and attitude to learning grades may also be summarised and reported to governors and other audiences.

7.5.3 Useful reports that an assessment database should include:

Progress matrices: A simple grid that compares pupils' latest assessments to those made at a previous point can help quickly spot those pupils that are not where you might expect them to be. Matrices can also be used to compare different types of data from a single point in time – for example, the latest teacher assessment against a recent test score – or compare current attainment to a target.

Y6 Sum Main Assessment

Y2 Sum SAT TA		Below	Towards	Within	Above
	WTS	Pupil Premium: 1 pupil (4%) ● Pupil-001	Pupil Premium: 1 pupil (4%) ● Pupil-004	Not Pupil Premium: 3 pupils (13%) ◎ Pupil-002 ◎ Pupil-007 ◎ Pupil-021 Pupil Premium: 1 pupil (4%) ● Pupil-009	
	EXS	Not Pupil Premium: 1 pupil (4%) ◎ Pupil-010	Not Pupil Premium: 1 pupil (4%) ◎ Pupil-019	Not Pupil Premium: 8 pupils (35%) ◎ Pupil-003 ◎ Pupil-005 ◎ Pupil-008 ◎ Pupil-011 ◎ Pupil-014 ◎ Pupil-016 ◎ Pupil-022 ◎ Pupil-023 Pupil Premium: 2 pupils (9%) ● Pupil-006 ● Pupil-015	Pupil Premium: 1 pupil (4%) ● Pupil-017
	GDS			Not Pupil Premium: 2 pupils (9%) ◎ Pupil-012 ◎ Pupil-018	Not Pupil Premium: 2 pupils (9%) ◎ Pupil-013 ◎ Pupil-020

Figure 7.1. Simple progress matrix comparing Year 6 pupils' current attainment to their results at Key Stage 1 (Summer, Year 2). We can see that most pupils have maintained standards and four of the pupils that were previously 'working towards' are now working within expectations. Pupils are grouped to make it easier to identify those in receipt of Pupil Premium funding.

Source: Insight.

Bar charts: Comparing a series of results is always useful, but stacked bar charts that allow comparison of the proportions of pupils working below, at and above expectations provide a more detailed picture of standards across a school.

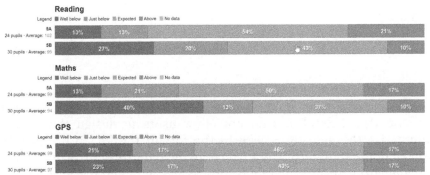

Figure 7.2. Stacked bar charts showing a summary of the results of standardised tests in reading, maths, and grammar, punctuation and spelling (GPS). The data is grouped by class and reveals that there is a higher proportion of pupils working below expectations in class 5B.

Source: Insight.

Scatter plots: When dealing with test scores, scatter plots are a must. They show the correlation – if any – between the results of two tests and – where correlation is high – can be used to predict future results. Dividing a scatter plot into quadrants will identify those pupils with consistently high or low scores on both tests, as well as those with high scores on one and low scores on another.

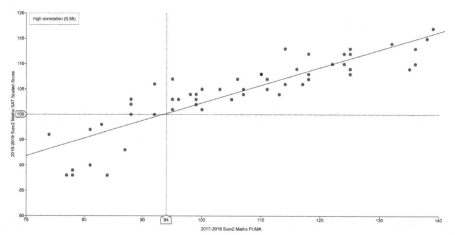

Figure. 7.3. Scatter plot comparing results of standardised tests taken in Year 5 against final Key Stage 2 results taken in Year 6. The correlation between the two tests is high and a score of 94 on the former test could be used as a predictor of expected standards (score of 100) on the latter. All pupils that achieved a good score (>=94) on the Year 5 test achieved expected standards at Key Stage 2. Five pupils that achieved a lower score (<94) in the Year 5 test went on to achieve expected standards.

Source: Insight.

Tables: Sometimes all you want is a table of numbers that shows, for example, percentages that are on track to meet targets in each subject. Unfortunately, many assessment databases do not allow users to design their own reports to summarise the data they need in the format they need it. They therefore resort to running numerous reports, copying data to their own templates, and even calculating results manually. An assessment database should let users build their own tables, specifying what data is included, and how that data is presented.

Dataproof Your School

	Reading			
	Main Assessment	**Age**	**Standardised Test**	**Phonics Score**
	% of pupils Expected or higher	Average Attainment	Average Attainment	Average Attainment
All Pupils	71%	6y 1m	98	34
Boys	79%	6y 1m	99	34
Girls	63%	6y 1m	97	34
Pupil Premium	56%	6y 8m	102	33
Not Pupil Premium	74%	6y 0m	97	34
Pupils with SEND	33%	5y 11m	83	31
Pupils without SEND	78%	6y 1m	100	35
EAL	64%	6y 1m	95	33
Not EAL	73%	6y 1m	98	34
High Attainers	88%	6y 11m	113	37
Middle Attainers	70%	6y 0m	96	34
Low Attainers	0%	4y 1m	74	32
Attendance is 0-89%	75%	6y 6m	101	34
Attendance is 90-100%	71%	6y 0m	97	34

Figure 7.4. A range of assessment averages for a Year 1 cohort broken down into various pupil groups. Whilst data in this format is desirable – and maybe useful in certain circumstances – please note the caveats discussed in section 7.4.1.7 and elsewhere in this book.

Source: Insight.

Venn diagrams: These are intuitive tools that are particularly useful for spotting pupils that are or are not working at a consistent standard across subjects. As with progress matrices, teachers may spend hours producing these manually. Having a system that can create Venn diagrams at the click of a button is therefore extremely welcome.

7.6 Reporting to parents

Often a manual process done in an application like Word, but one that can be assisted by technology and an assessment database can take much of the pain out of the task. Teachers' comments can be stored alongside assessment data and other

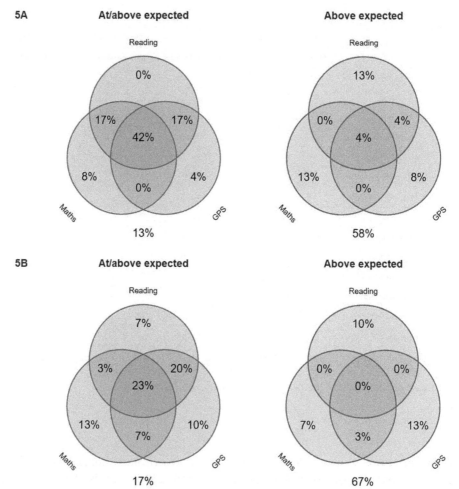

Figure 7.5. Venn diagrams showing combined attainment for two Year 5 classes. The disparity between classes is obvious, with nearly twice as many meeting expectations in 5A as in 5B.

Source: Insight.

key information in a single system, compiled into a school-designed template, and batch exported for printing or emailing to parents. We will return to the subject of what and how to report to parents in Chapter 9.

7.7 The school data ecosystem

An assessment database is not an island; it is part of a wider, integrated network of systems that perform important tasks, the data from which will feed into the assessment database. An integrated assessment network may therefore look something like this:

7.7.1 Management Information System (MIS)

The MIS is the most important system used in a school. It contains vital pupil information, including attendance, prior attainment history and exam registration details, and is used to prepare statutory returns to the government. Pupil information is transferred from the MIS to the assessment database to add context to attainment records. If the school uses the assessment module packaged with their MIS – assuming it has the analysis functions listed above – then this is taken care of. Otherwise, check how your assessment database integrates with the MIS to ensure it is capable of storing the essential contextual information detailed in this chapter.

7.7.2 Proprietary Question Level Analysis (QLA) tools

Many providers of standardised tests – NFER and Rising Stars for example – also offer tools to analyse the results. Either online or in the form of a spreadsheet, these systems compare responses at item and domain level to those of the sample to reveal gaps and give an indication of school standards. It should be noted that manual entry of question-level data is time consuming and schools need to carefully consider the added benefit of this data. It is also important that standardised scores and assessment ages generated by these systems can be easily exported to the assessment database for further analysis.

7.7.3 Comparative judgement

This is a quick and robust solution to the challenges of assessing writing and an alternative to traditional moderation methods, comparative judgement systems – such as that provided by No More Marking – provide scaled scores, writing ages, and – in primary – an indication of expected standards and greater depth. Again, the output should be imported into your assessment database for comparison with latest national figures, targets, and results of previous assessments.

7.7.4 Question banks

Systems such as Carousel provide banks of questions that teachers can add to and draw on to create their own tests, and that pupils can use to test themselves. Using such tools can be a significant time saver and may also replace some standardised tests, which are useful for ascertaining a pupil's position in the national cohort but are not so effective at testing their knowledge of what has been taught. Results could be pulled into the assessment database for monitoring over time and comparing to other data such as the scores from standardised tests.

7.7.5 Target setting

In England and Wales, many schools use FFT to generate estimated grades based on pupils' prior attainment. If your school uses this or a similar system, ensure your assessment database is capable of importing the data for comparison with other assessments.

7.7.6 Provision mapping

This is a tool predominantly for mapping the support provided to pupils with special educational needs, but one that has wider application. It should enable the setting and monitoring of individual targets and provide a facility to link types of provision to the pupils concerned in order to track the effectiveness of support, including the cost element. Often this is done in a spreadsheet or in a standalone system, but integrating provision mapping into the main assessment databases is desirable because it avoids the need to transfer data and cross-reference one system with another. Provision mapping is discussed in more detail in Chapter 6.

7.8 Summary

An assessment database is a powerful – and essential – tool for any school. It may not perform all the functions outlined in this chapter, but we must at least aim to have a reliable, accessible system that ensures data is recorded once and used many times to inform key audiences and build that all-important picture of learning over time. We must stop conflating 'tracking' with assessment, and viewing the primary purpose of an assessment database as a tool for measuring progress in simple, linear terms.

Schools also need to stop relying on 'tracking systems' to provide auto-generated grades for pupils based on the number of learning objectives checked off a list. These are not assessment systems – they do not assess pupils – they are databases: libraries of useful information with various tools that should make the analysis, presentation and reporting of data a straightforward task.

References

Commission on Assessment without Levels (2015) *Commission on Assessment without Levels: Final Report* [Online]. Available at: https://assets.publishing.service.gov.uk/government/uploads/system/uploads/attachment_data/file/483058/Commission_on_Assessment_Without_Levels_-_report.pdf (Accessed on 4 May 2021) p. 32.

Spielman, A. (2018) Amanda Spielman at the Bryanston Education Summit [Online]. Available at: www.gov.uk/government/speeches/amanda-spielman-at-the-bryanston-education-summit (Accessed 5 May 2021).

Teacher Workload Advisory Group (2018) *Making Data Work: Report of the Teacher Workload Advisory Group* [Online]. Available at: https://assets.publishing.service.gov.uk/government/uploads/system/uploads/attachment_data/file/754349/Workload_Advisory_Group-report.pdf (Accessed 4 May 2021).

Some useful websites:

Powerful and customisable online assessment database for primary schools: www.insighttracking.com/

Data analysis and benchmarking for primary and secondary schools: https://fft.org.uk/

Assessment design and standardisation for Multi-Academy Trusts: www.smartgrade.co.uk/

Online question bank to help students embed knowledge: www.carousel-learning.com/

Comparative judgement system that offers robust alternative to traditional moderation: www.nomoremarking.com/

DEVELOPING A DATA STRATEGY

8

Taking control of your data is likely to be a challenging, though rewarding, process. The legacy of previous administrations, superseded accountability frameworks and decades of misuse and misunderstanding of school data are likely to have created a complicated landscape both in your school and your local networks. Your place within your management structure will have a significant impact on the way you develop your data strategy; others will have their own views as to the best way to use data in education which may not align with your own – at least, not yet.

Developing a clear strategy for your use of data will enable you to manage the change process. In this chapter, we will walk you through the process of dataproofing your school.

8.1   Establish the need to take control of your data

As you saw in Chapter 2, schools have a licence to change when it comes to pupil data. By now, you will have begun to understand the need to take control of your data. In brief, both external and internal pressures have distorted the understanding of the benefits – and shortcomings – of using data in schools. There will be many stakeholders who have yet to realise the extent of the problem.

The governmental bodies responsible for education have driven much of the use of data in the education system. The good news is that they have changed their position radically in the past few years. Whereas bodies such as Ofsted used to place high value on numerical data generated by schools, they currently disregard any internal data used in schools and only use statutory data in specific and limited ways.

Despite this change, many schools continue to use data in ways which are questionable at best. Assumptions based on extremely low-quality data are rife. Too much time is spent generating and collating data that is largely meaningless and certainly has little or no effect on any learner's experience in school. Systems for processing and storing data often have huge impacts on workload, whilst simultaneously distorting the understanding of the benefits of using information to support the work we do in schools.

Information is often analysed in a superficial way which does little or nothing to inform decisions that might impact on learners' experiences in school.

To take control, schools need to think strategically about their use of data.

Ten steps to creating a successful data strategy

In this section, we will look at the ten steps needed to create a successful data strategy, which are outlined below:

1. Establish the need to take control of your data
2. Develop an initial audit to assess the situation in your organisation
3. Establish an outline plan to develop a data strategy
4. Involve stakeholders in factual briefing events
5. Audit the current use of data in your organisation
6. Develop Common Data protocols
7. Manage ongoing stakeholder development
8. Develop your initial data strategy document
9. Develop one-year, three-year and ten-year plans
10. Adapt and change as you take control of your data.

Step 1: Establish the need to take control of your data

This book should provide you with all you need to understand to take control of your data. Chapter 2 in particular should provide you with plenty food for thought, when you consider both the external and internal pressures on school data as well as the issues with and impact of progress measures over the years. It will also help you to question the way in which you have stored data and to consider how you should respond to the changes in the expectations of the external accountability systems. You may have a lot to do or you may be well on your way to having taken control of your data; either way, you need to be sure why you are embarking on the process in order for it to be a success.

Both the school system and the accountability frameworks under which schools operate have changed dramatically over the years. As a result, those working in any school organisation will have had a mixture of experiences, training and direction when it comes to understanding, interpreting and acting on insights from data. Without a clear understanding of the landscape within which you operate, you are likely to find that any programme of change is delayed by misunderstandings or derailments which you uncover as you move forward.

It is crucial, therefore, that the main decision makers in your organisation are involved in scoping your data strategy development from as early a stage as possible, and that they are clear that the process will involve significant challenge as you take control of your data.

In the majority of cases, you will find that data has been seen as a tool to measure pupil progress or as a tool to measure teacher performance – and in many cases, as a mixture of both. Data will have been misinterpreted, or misunderstood, and collecting data will have become an end in itself, rather than a means to an end.

A dataproof school is one in which the benefits and dangers of collating data are well understood, and all of those involved in generating, collating, analysing and acting on data have a clear understanding of the purpose and scope of each stage of the data-management process. It is crucial that this is established before you move to the next phase, as the more clear you are about what you are aiming to achieve from the outset of the journey, the more likely it is that you will take control of your data effectively and efficiently.

Step 2: Develop an initial audit to assess the situation in your organisation

To understand the systems currently in place, you will need to identify the key stakeholders involved in the audit and development process. You are likely to identify your school leadership team(s), your wider networks (particularly if you are part of a Multi-Academy Trust or a wider grouping of schools), your data managers if you have them, and those who are likely to generate and use school data – your teaching teams. Depending on your situation, you may wish to involve other groups, such as governors or parent representatives, in the audit process.

Once you have identified your key stakeholders, you will need to involve the group in the initial phase of your data strategy project. You should advise the group that you are embarking on a project to develop and implement a data strategy for your organisation, and that the project aims to create a strategic framework for the use of data to support your educational aims.

By auditing stakeholder understanding of the following broad areas, you will begin to understand the strengths, weaknesses, opportunities and threats within your organisation:

- Any immediate areas of concern
- The quality of current and historical assessment data
- The effectiveness of current data systems, including the assessment database
- The efficiency of current data gathering, collating and analysis
- The robustness of actions resulting from data gathering, collating and analysis.

You may also wish to gather views on the following:

- Teaching staff's data literacy
- Governor and Senior Leadership Team data literacy.

Data literacy involves the understanding of the strengths and weaknesses of attainment, contextual and development (or progress) data.

The initial stakeholder audit process should be as open as possible so that all of those involved are able to raise any issues. As ever in any change process, it is much better to understand concerns from the outset rather than have concerns emerge slowly over time. Of course, some issues will arise in the initial stage of the process; the aim is to have allowed as much as possible to emerge in the stage prior to the roll out of the data strategy which you are going to develop.

Step 3: Establish an outline plan to develop a data strategy

Once you have undertaken your initial data gathering, you will be in a position to plan your data strategy. This is a two-stage process: the first part is to address the areas you have identified in the audit/scoping process and to develop and implement protocols for gathering, collating, analysing and acting on data; the second part is to create a roadmap for the subsequent use of data within your school or wider organisation.

Your outline plan for the initial stage should take into account your understanding of the time required to develop and implement protocols for gathering the high-quality data you need. You will need to undertake factual briefing events and to audit the current use of data in your organisation in order for your key stakeholders to fully participate in the development of your data strategy.

As well as including time for the development of protocols for data generation, your outline plan for the initial stage of the process will need to include work to develop your assessment database. Chapter 7 includes the detail you require here to understand both where you currently are and where you need to aim to be.

Finally, the initial stage will need to include time to create a roadmap for the subsequent use of data within your school or wider organisation, which we will return to in Step 8.

Step 4: Involve stakeholders in factual briefing events

Step 2 of the data strategy development process is likely to have revealed areas that will need to be addressed via factual briefing events. Chapters 3 and 4 on high-quality data and standardised tests should prove useful here, as will a briefing that explains the issues we have identified in Chapter 2 on distortions. Chapter 5 on teacher assessment may be useful too, along with sections in Chapter 6 on assessing outliers.

Step 5: Audit the current use of data in your organisation

Following your factual briefing events, you need to establish exactly how the land currently lies. You need to understand what systems are in place, what the stakeholders involved think about the generation, collation and analysis of data (especially in the light of the factual briefing events in Step 4), and what actions currently result from the activity at present taking place. The most effective way to establish the situation is to identify your key stakeholders and to open up discussions with them, creating channels of communication which will allow everyone to be involved with the development of an effective data strategy. This is likely to involve setting up a working party or pilot group, particularly if your organisation includes a number of schools.

As you have seen from Chapters 1 and 3, we broadly group data into four categories: contextual information, attainment data, development and additional provision. Your audit gives you an opportunity to introduce these groupings and to explore each area with the relevant stakeholders.

You may also want to explore the quality of data which is currently generated, to find if there are any insights which your stakeholders might have as to how accurate the data currently gathered is (and to explore beliefs about accuracy of data, bearing in mind what you have understood from Chapter 3 on high-quality data).

The audit also gives you an opportunity to explore the process for collation and analysis of data; who does this, how efficient is it, what analysis is undertaken and how effective it is. This part of the audit allows you to gather information which will feed into the next step of the process when you begin to develop an outline plan to develop a data strategy.

Finally, the audit should also gather information on the outcomes of the data gathering, collation and analysis – what happens as a result of the information the school holds.

Step 6: Develop Common Data protocols

Once you have established what data is currently being collated, you can begin to develop protocols for the data which you will gather under your new data strategy. As you will see in Chapter 3, to dataproof your school, you need to gather information which will allow you to build up a picture of each learner's needs. Your context will drive your Common Data protocols. Every organisation will have a slightly different set of demands, and whilst these are likely to change over time, you should develop Common Data protocols that reflect where you are now.

As you will appreciate by now, all data has a cost in time and effort, and your Common Data should aim to minimise costs whilst maintaining effectiveness.

Box 8.1

Examples of Common Data for which to develop protocols

Primary

Attainment data

- EYFSP/PSC/KS1 data
- Results of Standardised Tests
- Ongoing teacher assessments
- Year 4 Multiplication Tables Check scores

Contextual data

- Attendance
- SEND status
- Free School Meals status
- EAL status
- Date/Term of Birth
- Children Looked After

Development data

- Receiving Intervention (with details at child level)

(Continued)

- Mobility (with details)
- Start date
- Barriers to Learning (with details)
- Engagement score (Teacher assessed on a 1–5 scale)
- Behaviour score (Teacher assessed on a 1–5 scale)
- Teachers/Year (numerical)

Secondary

Attainment data

- PSC/ Year 4 Multiplication Tables Check scores/KS2 data
- Year 7 Baseline assessments (CATs, etc.)
- Ongoing teacher assessments
- In-house test data
- Annual Maths and Reading Standardised Scores
- Targets and estimates

Contextual data

- Attendance
- SEND status
- Free School Meals status
- EAL status
- Date/Term of Birth
- Children Looked After

Development data

- Receiving Intervention (with details at child level)
- Mobility (with details)
- Start date
- Barriers to Learning (with details)
- Engagement score (Teacher assessed on a 1–5 scale)
- Behaviour score (Teacher assessed on a 1–5 scale)
- Teachers/Year (numerical)

Once you have identified which Common Data you wish to collate, you will need to create clear protocols to indicate when and how it should be gathered. It is crucial that the protocols are standardised as much as possible so that any bias is minimised in future analysis you undertake. It would not make sense to compare data gathered in October to that gathered in May, for example, as any number of factors could influence what is collected at each point in time.

As a rule of thumb, protocols should be written so that they can be read and clearly understood by new members of staff – they should not rely on any previous knowledge which is not part of your overall data strategy.

You should aim to gather data once in an academic year. Once your data strategy is embedded, this will provide the information required to group children into those who do and do not require additional support. Remember that the recommendation from the *Making Data Work* report (DfE, 2018: 11) is that schools should not 'have more than two or three attainment data collection points a year, which should be used to inform clear actions'.

Whilst you may wish to gather attainment data more than once in an academic year in the early stages of your data strategy, you should ensure that your ongoing analysis of your data should aim to establish whether multiple data points per year add to your understanding of learners' needs. If they do, you may wish to gather attainment data two or three times a year. If they do not, you should gather attainment data once a year.

As part of your Common Data proposals, you should include details of the way in which you will group pupils under your new data strategy. As a dataproof school, your aim is to identify which pupils do and do not require additional support. As such, we recommend that you aim to create two broad groupings:

- Pupils requiring support
- Pupils who do not require support.

You may wish to divide the 'Pupils Requiring Support' into categories for pupils with identified SEND and those for whom some additional support is required. You may also wish to have a group of higher achievers for whom you may provide additional provision. Some examples are provided in Chapter 9.

Step 7: Manage ongoing stakeholder development

Once you have developed your Common Data protocols, you will need to share them with your working party and the wider organisation as appropriate. It is likely that you will need to ensure that channels of communication are open and that stakeholders can feed back any concerns they might have at this point. As this is the first point at which the shape of the future direction of your data strategy will become clear – and the impact it will have on those who are wedded to their existing practice – it is likely that some stakeholders may push back against the Common Data protocols.

Some stakeholders may wish to retain a focus on measuring 'pupil progress', despite the evident issues we explored in Chapter 2. You may find the *Making Data Work* report useful here. You may also find that some stakeholders may be wedded to their existing assessment practices. It should be made clear to teaching teams that they are free to gather and collate any data which they find useful to support their practice. This might be above and beyond what is asked of them in the Common Data protocols and it is important that you ensure that additional procedures are in line with the principles set out in your data strategy.

Where your Common Data protocols ask more of your teaching teams than their current practice, you should consider phasing in the protocols over time so that any issues can be dealt with before you move to the next phase of your data development. This may be the case if you intend to introduce new standardised tests or to formalise practice across multiple classes, year groups or schools.

Always remember that the intention is to create a data strategy that will deliver maximum benefit in five to ten years; the more you can ensure that the foundations of your strategy are embedded from the outset, the greater the likelihood that your strategy will be effective.

Step 8: Develop your initial data strategy document

Whilst most schools work within a policy framework, it is important to note that dataproof schools have an underlying strategy which informs policies. Your data strategy document will ensure that both existing and future members of staff are clear as to the intent and implementation of your use of data to inform practice.

A data strategy should start with the aims of the strategy. This may ultimately be as simple as, 'We use data to inform decisions which provide additional support to cohorts, classes, groups and individuals'. In the first few years of the data strategy, it may be more developmental: 'In order to provide high-quality information to enable decisions to be made to provide additional support to cohorts, classes, groups and individuals, we aim to standardise our data gathering, collation and analysis so that we build pictures of need across our school/organisation.'

Once you have identified the aims of your data strategy, you can create a roadmap to achieve those aims. This should include the development and implementation of Common Data protocols, training and support (for both new members of staff and ongoing support for those responsible for data), as well as the outline one-year, three-year and ten-year plans for your use of data.

Once the initial document has been shared and agreed, it should be used to inform updates of those school policies which reference pupil data.

Step 9: Develop one-year, three-year and ten-year plans

Your initial data strategy document will contain outlines of your short-, medium- and long-term plans; once your initial strategy document has been agreed and put in place, you should begin to formalise your developmental plans. Assuming that you are starting from scratch, you will need to ensure that the plans include the following:

One-year plan

You will need to identify actions for the next academic year in your one-year plan. These may be actions for gathering, collating or analysing data, depending on your context.

Planning for gathering and collating pupil assessment data

If you do not have protocols for in-school assessment data, this should be in your one-year plan. Pupil assessment data can be split into existing statutory data and in-school data.

Existing statutory data should be recorded in a standardised format as defined in your Common Data protocols. If you have not defined a standardised format for this data as yet, the development of these protocols should be in your one-year plan.

Where you need to introduce new in-school pupil assessment data, you should include this in your one-year plan. You need to develop and formalise the protocols for gathering and collating this data, ensuring that the arrangements implemented in the first year can be replicated in future years.

Planning for analysing data

Pupil data will be used to inform identification of cohorts, classes, groups and individuals in need of additional support. This process should be driven by teaching teams with close support and assistance from senior leadership. In your one-year plan, you should develop or implement the protocols for analysing data. Ultimately, this should take place in regular pupil development discussions; in your one-year plan you should state how often these discussions will take place. As your strategic use of data becomes embedded, these discussions are likely to reduce in frequency for most children and classes as your picture of the needs of your pupils builds up.

You should consider how best to support the cohort at the point of entry to your school; whilst you will have access to data for this year group, it will be somewhat different from the Common Data which will be gathered in subsequent years. In the first year of your data strategy, you should work with your 'entrance' team to develop protocols for the data which you will gather and collate for this year group.

Planning for actions resulting from analysis of data

In your first year, you should review how additional support is managed, and consider how this might develop as your data becomes more meaningful.

Three-year plan

Your three-year plan should focus on ensuring that your strategic use of data becomes embedded. You should plan regular training and support for the effective gathering, collation and analysis of data. Actions resulting from your analysis should become more focused, along with effective use of data to monitor the impact of targeted support which is put in place.

All staff who are responsible for the gathering, collation and analysis of data should have annual refreshers in data literacy. This will develop over the three-year period, but may include CPD on standardised test development, essential psychometrics, research reviews, reading groups and so on. New staff should be supported to ensure that they are able to access previous training materials.

Over the medium term, you should aim to develop the actions taken as a result of the improved understanding of the cohorts, classes, groups and individuals in your school. You should build up a picture of the support that has been put in place in previous years – its effectiveness, cost (particularly in time and effort) and impact; this will enable tighter targeting of future support and inform support for pupils as they move into year groups which have had support in previous years.

Where you are rolling out a programme of newly introduced standardised tests over multiple years, this should be included in your three-year plan.

Remember not to add further actions simply because you have more capacity as elements of your data use become more embedded and less time consuming – your aim is to reduce the time and effort spent on managing and using data as your school becomes more dataproof.

Dataproof Your School

Ten-year plan

Ultimately, your aim is for your school to become dataproof. All the data gathered, collated and analysed centrally must result in concrete actions to support learning in your school. Each stage of the process of gathering, collating and analysing data should be streamlined as much as possible whilst maintaining high standards to ensure that any activity involving data is worth doing.

Your ten-year plan, therefore, should include actions to minimise the time and effort taken to gather, collate and analyse data. Teachers of classes that have been in your school for several years should have an extremely detailed picture of needs of the pupils they teach; every additional year should add meaningful data which adds further detail. Those teaching 'entrance' years should gather data which is known to be useful.

Step 10: Adapt and change as you take control of your data

As should be clear from the outline ten-year plan in Step 9, the ultimate aim is to ensure that as little time as possible is spent on gathering, collating and analysing data – schools should focus on teaching rather than crunching numbers. It is crucial, therefore, that you constantly review what you are doing to ensure that your management and use of data is as efficient as it can be.

This should mean that you are always open to change which will improve your use of data; this might involve adapting to new types of assessment, or systems for storing and managing data, or it might involve utilising new ways of gathering data from pupils or teachers.

The Covid-19 shock of 2020–21 has shown how quickly schools can adapt to a changing situation, with schools utilising online platforms in new and exciting ways. Gathering information from pupils has become much more efficient, particularly from online platforms which have data gathering at their heart. You may wish to consider incorporating some of this data into your Common Data protocols as you move forward, for example. What is certain is that things will change and you should consider whether you wish to change your systems in the light of that change.

Taking control of your data as a dataproof school means that you can develop your one-, three- and ten-year plans as you move forward, always thinking strategically about your use of data.

A data strategy checklist

Table 8.1 shows a data strategy checklist that you can use.

Table 8.1. A data strategy checklist.

Step	Action	Who is involved?	Duration	Date started	Date completed
1	Establish the need to take control of your data	Main decision makers	1–3 months		
2	Develop an initial audit to assess the situation in your organisation	Key stakeholders	1 month		
3	Establish an outline plan to develop a data strategy	Project Manager	1 month		
4	Involve stakeholders in factual briefing events	All stakeholders	1 month		
5	Audit the current use of data in your organisation	Working party/ Pilot group	1 month		
6	Develop Common Data protocols	Project Manager	1 month		
7	Manage ongoing stakeholder development	All stakeholders	1–3 months		
8	Develop your initial data strategy document	Project Manager	1 month		
9	Develop one-year, three-year and ten-year plans	Project Manager	Ongoing		
10	Adapt and change as you take control of your data	Project Manager	Ongoing		

Summary

This chapter provides a step-by-step guide to developing and introducing a successful data strategy. It provides a concise summary of the process, which will help you as you take control of your data.

Reference

Department for Education (DfE) (2018) *Making Data Work*. London: DfE.

DATAPROOFING IN ACTION

9

9.1.   The dataproof philosophy

On 20 August 1980, the great Tyrolean climber Reinhold Messner stood on the summit of Everest. Considering the mountain had first been climbed 27 years previously, this may not seem like a significant achievement, but Messner's ascent was a watershed moment in the history of mountaineering: he climbed Everest solo and without the use of supplemental oxygen. It is widely regarded as one of the greatest ever feats of human endurance.

Up until that point, Himalayan expeditions were huge undertakings requiring military logistics, and the mountains were climbed using siege-style tactics. Large numbers of porters would ferry massive loads and construct sprawling base camps that were more like small villages. Teams of climbers supported by local Sherpa guides fixed lines higher and higher up the mountain to link a series of advanced camps stocked with supplies. Exhausted climbers would descend to base camp to recuperate, refreshed climbers would take over duties and, eventually, a team would be well placed to have a shot at reaching the summit.

But Messner was an alpinist – a purist in mountaineering terms. He had taken part in many siege-style expeditions and had already proved it was possible to climb Everest without bottled oxygen when he reached the summit with Peter Habeler in 1978. But climbing the world's highest mountain solo and in alpine style, without the security of fixed ropes, advanced camps and support teams, was another level entirely. Success – and survival – depended on speed and that would require a minimalist approach. The less he carried, the faster he could move; and the faster he moved, the less he would need to carry. This was very antithesis of siege-style expeditions.

Choosing a route on the less-frequented north side, Messner took only what he would need for a few days on the mountain, jettisoning any unnecessary weight to ensure he could move as fast as possible. It was a huge but calculated gamble, and it paid off. Previously, Everest had taken weeks if not months to climb; Messner was up and down in four days. His ascent changed high altitude mountaineering forever.

This alpine philosophy has wider application. Those that considered Messner's plan impossible were viewing it through the prism of standard practice that negated it. Sometimes, to advance and improve, we need to break the mould, turn things upside down, and do things that may seem counterintuitive. Maybe the things we deem vital are actually holding us back. Consider the issue of data collection in schools where too many teachers waste too much time gathering data of questionable value. Do we need to record assessments every half term for every subject, or track achievement against countless learning objectives, or input thousands of 1s and 0s into a question-level analysis tool? Do senior leaders need to prepare a 20-page data report for governors that compares the performance of every subgroup of pupils? Does any of this activity have a positive effect on pupils' outcomes, or are we simply collecting data to keep the wolf from the door? Without honest answers to these questions, schools cannot move on.

This book is a plea for data minimalism and a battle cry in the fight against the growing mountain of nonsense and unreasonable demands. Beyond statutory submissions, data collection must be proportionate, sustainable and justifiable in terms of the impact on teachers' workload, and this requires schools to 'Be ruthless: only collect what is needed to support outcomes for children' (Independent Teacher Workload Review Group, 2016). Data is an essential resource in the drive for school improvement, but we need to accept that there are limitations to what numbers can tell us and that the integrity of those numbers may be jeopardised by the pressure we place upon them. Always bear in mind that we want data to provide a warts-and-all picture, not a rose-tinted view.

Many years of data-driven accountability and performance management have taken their toll. Schools have become weighed down by the volume of data they collect, data that all too often lacks meaning, provides no real insight into children's learning, and therefore has little or no impact on outcomes. It is time to reassess the purpose of data, increase its value to teachers, and seek to do more with less.

Schools need a smaller data rucksack. They need to jettison excess baggage.

They need to be more Messner.

9.2. How to dataproof your school

Before we recap the main suggestions of this book, we need to take note of some golden rules. To dataproof your school, you need to do the following.

9.2.1 Stop using assessment data for performance management

As discussed in Chapter 2, for data to be useful it has to be as accurate as possible, and that requires minimising distorting factors as much as is practicable. Whether used directly in a classroom or indirectly in a meeting of senior leaders or governors, the primary purpose of assessment data collected in a school is to support children's learning; and anything that causes data to become distorted is therefore a risk to that purpose. Attempting to evaluate the performance of teachers on the basis of data they themselves are responsible for generating is highly likely to result in that data becoming compromised, which, in turn, is a clear and present danger to children's learning. In short, you can have accurate assessment data, or you can use it for performance management. The choice is yours.

9.2.2 Stop obsessing about measuring progress

Progress measures, which take pupils' start points into account, are seen as a fairer method of evaluating school performance than results alone; in England, metrics such as Key Stage 2 Value Added and Progress 8 scores have become dominant in recent years. Ostensibly, this is a good thing because schools are recognised for the distance children travel in their learning as well as for the grades they achieve, but these simplistic progress measures have caused numerous problems. In the pursuit of numbers that might emulate and predict national progress measures, schools have become distracted to the point where their internal assessment systems revolve around them. This has resulted in the invention of all manner of abstract approaches involving flightpaths of levels subdivided into as many units as are felt needed to show the progress required. It is perhaps inevitable that the most vulnerable schools have the most convoluted and incremental systems designed to 'prove' small steps of progress to whoever has oversight. But inventing more teacher assessment categories does not prove that pupils have made more progress; it just proves that someone has invented more teacher assessment categories. And using standardised tests to measure progress is not much better. Test scores are noisy, and you cannot subtract one score from another and treat the result as a measure of progress – that is not how they work. We need to be honest about progress measures, and their effect on assessment and workload: Are we inventing numbers to keep other people happy? Do those numbers have any impact on learning? And perhaps most importantly, is it really possible to measure progress anyway? Progress measures have a tendency to break assessment, and in England, this resulted in levels, P Scales and Development Matters age bands getting bent way beyond their elastic limit. Make sure the same does not happen to assessment in your school.

9.2.3 Stop collecting large volumes of low-value data

Too many teachers spend too much time generating data that has little or no effect on learning: recording teacher assessments in every subject every four to six weeks, constantly reviewing annual targets, entering thousands of 1s and 0s into question-level analysis systems, compiling journals of annotated photographic evidence of learning, and perhaps most pernicious of all, continually RAG-rating endless lists of learning objectives. All of these processes add significantly to teachers' already significant workload; time that would be better spent doing other, more impactful things. There is a balance to strike between the impact on learning and the impact on workload and we want to weight the scales in favour of the former. If they have a positive effect then carry on; if in doubt, leave it out.

9.2.4 Stop using overly complicated tracking systems

> Tracking software, which has been used widely as a tool for measuring progress with levels, cannot, and should not, be adapted to assess understanding of a curriculum that recognises depth and breadth of understanding as of equal value to linear progression. (Commission on Assessment without Levels, 2015)

Most schools have a tracking system, and they are undeniably useful – essential even – for the storage, retrieval and analysis of assessment data. But as discussed in Chapter 7, they should be viewed simply as that: assessment databases. Their elevation to oracle status has resulted in the proliferation of increasingly complicated systems that have become disconnected from the reality of the classroom – hundreds of report options that slice and dice the data in every way imaginable without necessarily providing any actionable information, just the comfort of numbers. If teachers are to spend hours feeding the machine, there has to be a benefit. Primarily, assessment databases are tools for storing useful information about pupils: their context, prior attainment, targets and recent assessment history alongside notes on any concerns, associated documents and information on additional provision that has been put in place. Summary data provided to governing bodies and the like should be a by-product of a system built to accommodate the school's assessment policy and support teachers in the classroom; it should not be the starting point that dictates system design. In short, assessment databases should be simple, accessible, secure and capable of storing any data in any format.

9.2.5 Stop making stuff up

Ultimately, this is what it all comes down to. Take an objective view of the data in your school and, as always, be honest about its purpose and value. If data provides insight and effects change, then carry on; if not, stop collecting it. In some schools it is inertia that prevents a shift in approach, in others it is outside pressure to report in a particular format to a specified timetable; but either way, 'there is no point in collecting "data" that provides no information about genuine learning' (Independent Teacher Workload Review Group, 2016). If you are having discussions about pupils progressing from band 4ee+ to 5e– and making 3.5 steps of progress over the last term, then it is probably time for a rethink. Be brave.

9.3 Frequency of data collection

There is generally no need to collect assessment data more than three times per year, and this may be reduced to just once a year for the majority of pupils in a truly dataproof school. It is worth noting that Ofsted, diverging from their previous reliance on internal data, are now investigating how the frequent collection of large volumes of data affects teacher workload. Drawing on the recommendations of the Teacher Workload Advisory Group's 2018 *Making Data Work* report, *The School Inspection Handbook* now states that

> Schools choosing to use more than two or three data collection points a year should have clear reasoning for what interpretations and actions are informed by the frequency of collection; the time taken to set assessments, collate, analyse and interpret the data; and the time taken to then act on the findings. If a school's system for data collection is disproportionate, inefficient, or unsustainable for staff, inspectors will reflect this in their reporting on the school. (Ofsted, 2021)

Always consider the reasons for collecting data.

Box 9.1

We need to talk about targets

There is a concept in urban design known as shared space. It involves the removal of much of the street furniture – signage, painted lines, bollards, traffic lights and barriers – to improve safety. The boundaries between the different zones of use – for pedestrians, bikes and cars – are blurred, and road users become more attentive as a result. Think about that: removing the paraphernalia that are designed to keep us safe can actually makes us safer. Sometimes systems and practices we believe to be vital can result in the opposite to the intended effect, but we have become too entrenched in our ways to see it. We need to consider the possibility that targets set for pupils – ubiquitous in schools – are a problem and may even be 'dangerous nonsense' (Newmark, 2017).

When determining the value of targets, there are three 'P's to bear in mind: purpose, prediction and probability.

Purpose

Why set targets for individual pupils? Be honest. If their impact on learning and outcomes is indisputably positive, then keep setting them. But are there any negative side effects? Can they lower expectations, seem unachievable, or appear to be a fait accompli?

And if targets are more for measuring teachers' performance, then we have to consider the dangers involved (see Chapter 2: distortions). First, is it fair to hold certain teachers to a higher standard because they happen to be teaching an exam year? Then recognise that any attempt to apply the same standards across the school will ramp up the stakes of other forms of assessment. Increased test preparation is inevitable in the lead up to national examinations, but is it beneficial in other years, too? Do we want to turn ostensibly low stakes assessments into something of far greater significance by linking them to teachers' performance management and risk the artificial inflation of results in the process?

Finally, if individual targets stem from disaggregating a whole school target linked to an external measure of school performance, then are the desires of students – who might prefer one course over another – pitted against those of the school that wants to maximise its results? This is perhaps a sad inevitability in these times of heightened accountability, but it is certainly something to reflect on.

Prediction

Having set a target, how do we predict if pupils are on track to achieve them? In schools in England, it is inevitable that students will be set targets in the form of GCSE grades

(Continued)

when studying in Key Stage 4, and that teachers will be capable of predicting outcomes with reasonable success. But is it appropriate to set GCSE grade targets for pupils in Key Stage 3, who are not yet on GCSE courses? This can lead to the invention of metrics and flightpaths in a vain attempt to track each pupil's progress towards their targets. Pretending a pupil is working at an unsubstantiated grade that sits on a straight line drawn between two arbitrary points is probably not helpful.

And what about targets in primary schools? In England, these could take the form of either a fine-scaled score or a broad grade. Both are fairly pointless. The fine-scaled score is usually derived from a value-added calculation and represents the break-even point: the score the pupil needs to achieve on a test to secure at least a zero progress score so as not to put a dent in whole school measures. There are two problems here: 1) not everyone can achieve those scores (see probability, below), and 2) the scores cannot be predicted. If a pupil has a 50/50 chance of achieving a score of 103 or more in a test, and you cannot predict what score the pupil is likely to achieve, then it's not a very useful target.

This brings us on to setting broad grades instead. But the vast majority of pupils in primary schools – some pupils with special needs aside – are working through the same curriculum content towards the same aim: to be ready for secondary education. One could argue that there should just be one target for all pupils regardless of start point: to meet expected standards. Indeed, many primary headteachers eschew individual targets in favour of exactly that approach, and one reduced the target-setting section of their school's self-evaluation to a single sentence: 'All pupils that sit Key Stage 2 tests will meet expected standards.'

Probability

Many schools set targets based on estimates that are derived from pupils' prior attainment. Estimates are an expression of probability; unfortunately, they are too often viewed as minimum expectations. A pupil may have a 60% chance of achieving a particular grade or above because 60% of pupils with the same prior attainment did so in previous years nationally. This of course means there is a 40% chance of falling short of that grade. Pupils with higher prior attainment have a greater chance of achieving a particular grade than those with lower prior attainment but it is never certain and, as such, estimates should be treated in the same way as betting odds. Estimates provide useful indicators of possible results, but it is essential that schools understand how they are calculated before adopting them as targets. If all schools set targets based on estimates calculated from pupils' prior attainment, then half of them will be disappointed. And that will only be exacerbated if everyone is aiming to be in the top 20%. Always take note of the probability; don't just look at the grade.

Key questions

Target setting ceased to be statutory in England in 2010 and is now purely an internal decision.

The assessment frameworks used by St Ralph Sherwin CMAT, produced in conjunction with Lee Northern at E-ACT, state that:

Individual pupil targets should never be used in Early Years or in key stages 1, 2 [or 3]. There is considerable evidence of the negative impact of target setting on pupils' achievement and expectations of themselves, as well as teachers' expectations. Targets at a pupil level often lack validity and reliability and are sometimes derived from the inappropriate use of baseline measures. (St Ralph Sherwin CMAT, 2020 (unpublished))

Therefore, before setting targets you should consider the following questions:

1. What is the purpose of targets?
2. How will you predict if pupils are on track to achieve them?
3. What is the probability of a target being met?

9.4 How to simplify your teacher assessment

One of the reasons for the removal of levels from the national curriculum in England was that they had become too fragmented and provided no useful information. The misappropriation of levels for the purposes of accountability and measuring progress led to distortion, a breakdown into ever smaller subunits, and ultimately their demise. It was hoped that out of the ashes of levels, something more meaningful would grow. As discussed in Chapter 2, the opposite happened – things got a lot worse.

So, how should we record teacher assessment? In a word, simply. Avoid unsubstantiated metrics and ambiguous terms; avoid linear flightpaths and expected rates of progress; avoid inventing data to keep other people happy. Just record assessment as it is, using the sort of language you would use in the classroom. Start from there and work up, not from the outdated opinion of an advisor downwards.

Here are some suggestions.

9.4.1 Early Years

When Early Years practitioners talk of 'age-related expectations', they really mean it; in other years, the term is conflated with curriculum expectations, and this can cause problems. Assessment in the Early Years is, quite rightly, focused on a child's development with reference to their age. As such, you can have two children in the same class at very different stages of development that are both recorded as being 'at age-related expectations' because they were born at opposite ends of the academic year. A year gap makes a huge difference at such a young age.

Most schools in England use the Development Matters framework to inform Early Years judgements, which provides examples of typical development in each age band. The bands are deliberately broad and overlap but, inevitably, have been broken down into sublevels for the purpose of measuring progress. The crucial overlap has been completely ignored in pursuit of a neat metric and, as with levels, the system has become bent out of shape. This is one problem. The other problem is the conflict that arises when age-related assessment is used to track towards curriculum expectations such as the early learning goals. We could easily have summer-born pupils at a typical level of development for their age that are not on track to meet end-of-year expectations, which is not ideal when attempting to forecast standards.

Our suggestion is to scrap progress measures and associated bandings in favour of a clearer scheme that simply describes the child's development with reference to their age at each assessment point: *below typical*, *typical*, *above typical* for example.

In the reception year, with the Early Years Foundation Stage Profile statutory assessment looming, this could switch to a curriculum-focused assessment that describes whether or not pupils are on track to meet the early learning goals. This could simply be a binary *on track/not on track* option or a scheme more aligned with that used in other year groups: *working below*, *towards*, *within* and *above expectations*, for example. The latter is preferable for those that want greater differentiation and a common approach across the school.

To investigate whether age accounts for the disparities in development, assessment data can simply be grouped by month or term of birth in the assessment database.

9.4.2 Primary: Key Stages 1 and 2

This is much more straightforward. Ditch the flightpaths in favour of a simple assessment scheme that broadly describes pupils' security in the curriculum based on what has been taught so far. As described above, a model with four bands – along the lines of *working below*, *towards*, *within* and *above expectations* – will suffice. For foundation subjects, this may be further simplified to a binary '*meeting/not meeting expectations*' outcome. Such approaches – where pupils may be in the same band for extended periods – mean an end to progress measures, but they replace ambiguity with clarity and work well in a progress matrix-style report (see Chapter 7). The issues usually arise when trying to use data to differentiate pupils with special educational needs and show smaller steps of learning, which can easily lead back to a levels-style approach. For this group of diverse children, we need more suitable and insightful assessments and data, not a return to the linear progression assumptions of the past, and this is dealt with in detail in Chapter 6.

9.4.3 Secondary: Key Stage 3

Key Stage 3 is more complicated. Many, if not most, schools have implemented systems based on simplistic, straight line flightpaths that link arbitrary groupings of Key Stage 2 scores to final GCSE grades, and this leads to two broad approaches: 'working at' grades and 'working towards' grades. The former – the worst of the two options – is supposed to represent the grade the student might achieve if they were to sit the final exams now, whilst the latter – which seems more logical – is an indication of what they are on track to achieve when they take their final exams. 'Working at' grades provide the comfort of a progress measure – count the grades of progress over time; 'working towards' grades exist because targets are set from students' on-entry grades. They are exactly the sorts of approaches that the Commission on Assessment without Levels (2015) and the Independent Teacher Workload Review Group (2016) warned against, and neither are appropriate when the students concerned are not yet following GCSE courses (Benyohai, 2019).

A seemingly better option is to use a system such as that recommended above for Key Stages 1 and 2, but there are some problems when applied here. Unlike in primary schools, where pupils are in mixed ability classes and will typically work through the same curriculum towards a common set of expected standards, students in secondary schools will often be placed into sets for some subjects. This presents challenges when attempting to use a simple teacher assessment scheme. You could describe a student in a higher set as 'working towards' expectations, whilst a pupil in a lower set is recorded as 'working within' expectations. The latter therefore might appear to be at a higher 'level' of attainment than the former, but that is not the case when we consider the varying degrees of difficulty of what is being taught. Our scheme may therefore require an additional piece of information to indicate the pupil's set.

Alternatively, a completely different approach, involving the tracking of percentile rank position in the cohort, is worth considering. An on-entry assessment or Key

Stage 2 result will provide a baseline rank from which relative changes can be monitored. Tracking pupils' decile or quintile rank position may be preferable where a broader classification is desired.

9.4.4 Secondary: Key Stage 4

There is no escaping the fact that in Key Stage 4 students are on GCSE courses and schools will therefore want to record the grades that they are predicted to achieve alongside their targets. This is at least relevant and has some meaning, but progress measures based on supposedly current 'working at' grades are to be avoided, and it should be borne in mind that it is not appropriate to suggest a GCSE grade when the student is yet to finish the course.

9.5   Standardised tests

Standardised tests do not need to be administered every term for every year group and are not available for every subject, but they are very useful tools. They will give you a good idea of where pupils sit on a national attainment bell curve, but they are more limited in terms of their capacity to diagnose gaps in learning. Standardised tests are designed to assess a range of items that pupils of a particular age might know, and by comparing each pupil's result to the results of a national reference sample, they provide a pupil's rank position. This puts the attainment of a cohort in a national context, which will help us infer who is and is not on track to meet certain standards. Standardised tests are less useful, however, at revealing gaps in learning unless they are well aligned with the school's curriculum. This can be an issue with autumn and spring term tests, and is a particular problem in maths, the teaching of which may vary significantly from school to school.

Generally speaking, internally designed tests are better suited to the task of assessing pupils' knowledge and revealing gaps in their learning; standardised tests, on the other hand, perform the role of establishing pupils' national position. If pupils are achieving high scores on the former and low scores on the latter, this may suggest the school's curriculum is not challenging enough, or vice versa. It is also worth comparing the results of standardised tests with teacher assessments – teachers will often err on the side of caution despite pupils achieving above average test scores. In schools in more vulnerable situations, on the other hand, where teachers are held to account on the basis of their assessments, the opposite may happen. Cross-referencing standardised test scores with other forms of data can therefore be quite revealing.

Standardised tests provide schools with a huge amount of data: standardised scores, age standardised scores (standardised scores that have been adjusted to take account of a child's age in year), percentile rank and age equivalent scores. In addition, scores will often come with confidence intervals, which can help determine whether or not there is 'significant' difference between the results of consecutive tests: if confidence intervals overlap, this suggests that the change in score is not out of the ordinary; if there is no overlap then this might suggest a notable change in result.

Age equivalent scores, on the other hand, can be useful for evaluating the effectiveness of interventions involving the lowest attaining pupils. For example, reading ages improving by 12 months on average over the course of a 3-month period of support is perhaps strong evidence for the success of a strategy. Age data, which is readily understood, is suitable for reporting to parents, especially those of children with special educational needs, where finer detail on progress is desirable.

As always, however, we must bear in mind that the results of standardised tests are noisy and are heavily influenced by the pupils' mindset on the day and by the conditions in which the test is administered. For data to be useful, schools must minimise distorting factors, which includes standardising the conditions under which tests are taken. We must also accept the limitations of standardised tests – they are powerful tools, but they are not a panacea.

9.6 Internal tests

If you want to check pupils' knowledge and understanding of what has been taught, then your own tests will do a better job than standardised tests because they will be aligned with your school's curriculum. It is possible to standardise the scores of such tests so that the results convey a common meaning, but a percentage – which is a form of standardisation – will suffice in most cases. The difference here is that standardised tests are designed to rank pupils in order in a national context and will therefore have questions that very few pupils will be able to answer. Whilst you cannot expect all pupils to answer all questions correctly on a standardised test, that may be the expectation when it comes to other forms of tests, for example spelling or multiplication tables tests.

Groups of schools – multi-academy trusts, for example – can leverage their greater student numbers to standardise the results of internal tests because it is more reasonable to assume that the population is approximate to the national population. It is therefore possible to create quasi-nationally standardised tests for all subjects, not just those subjects – mainly English and maths – for which commercial tests are available. Pupils' results provide a rank position, which can be treated as a proxy for national rank and compared to the rank on entry and monitored over time. Such data can also help shore up grade predictions at Key Stage 4.

9.7 Comparative judgement

Comparative judgement involves comparing pieces of work to sort them into rank order and therefore differs from traditional forms of teacher assessment, which tend to rely on rubrics of performance criteria. This norm-referencing of teacher assessment effectively bridges the divide between standardised tests and criteria-driven approaches and solves many of the issues of subjectivity and bias that exist in the assessment of non-tested subjects such as writing. It can, of course, be done at class or cohort level, but this will lack national referencing. At scale, with a national database and an army of teachers comparing pieces of work, thousands of pupils can be efficiently and accurately ranked. Systems such as that developed by No More Marking make this a relatively straightforward process and have the benefit of providing nationally standardised scores and ages for set writing tasks, which will complement and help validate other forms of assessment. Comparative judgement is therefore well worth exploring if you want to improve assessment of non-tested subjects and gain valuable standardised data that can be used to monitor progress over time.

9.8 Pupils with SEND

For pupils with SEND that are working below curriculum expectations, schools can easily fall into the trap of reinventing some form of levels-based system because they want, or are under pressure to 'show small steps of progress'. It is important that this is avoided if it results in increasing workload without providing any useful data, and risks a situation where pupils are simply placed into certain assessment bands because teachers feel compelled to show an 'expected' amount of progress. But there is no expected rate of progress or unit of learning common to all pupils and this is especially the case for pupils with SEND. What might be considered good progress for one pupil is insufficient for another. It should be noted that such misinformed expectations of progression prompted the decision to remove P Scales and replace them with a more appropriate relative engagement model.

Teachers can make an assessment that denotes the year curriculum that the pupil is working within and this can be used as a broad indication of progress, but careful consideration must be given before appending such ambiguous terms as 'emerging', 'developing' or 'secure' to any curriculum year indicator. Can a Year 5 pupil with SEND be described as working securely within the Year 2 curriculum, or are they working within it in the broadest sense? And is it ever accurate to suggest that they are progressing through the Year 2 curriculum in a similar way to Year 2 pupils?

Whilst standardised assessment can play an important role in informing teacher judgements, diagnosing gaps in learning and monitoring progress, it is vital that the correct tools are used. Schools should not use tests intended for earlier year groups unless they will provide useful information about what pupils can and cannot do. Using a test designed for Year 2 pupils to assess a Year 5 pupil with SEND will not give accurate results. Rather, it will tell you where that Year 5 pupil, aged 9 or 10, ranks amongst the national cohort of children aged 6 and 7. If that particular test assesses exactly what you need to assess for that particular child, and the test is accessible to them, then go ahead and use it, but bear in mind that the scores it produces will not be meaningful.

Instead, consider using separate, more appropriate tests for pupils with SEND. Parallel tests, which are of comparable difficulty and are not designed to be used at specific points in time, are well suited for use at either end of a period of additional support. Online, adaptive tests, which continually adjust the questions according to previous answers, are better at assessing pupils at the extreme ends of the bell curve, are quick to administer and provide instant results. Both are better options than using tests intended for other year groups and will produce more accurate scores and reading ages, which can be reported to parents and used to monitor progress over time.

When it comes to data on children working well below the standards of the curriculum, the focus should be on individuals, not groups. Comparing the performance of various pupil groups has always been misleading and this is especially the case here. Some form of provision mapping where assessment data is placed in the context of individual targets, additional support, and the various factors that might affect achievement, is far more powerful for telling the story of each pupil's educational journey. Such an approach will help to demonstrate that progress is a relative concept.

9.9 Reporting to governors (and external agencies)

Judging by the volume of data that school governors are often confronted with, you would be forgiven for thinking this subject deserves a chapter to itself. Governors certainly need data; what they don't need is a mountain of it. Burying time-starved volunteers under an avalanche of data of dubious quality is counterproductive – the law of diminishing returns applies.

Until 2016, every school in England received an annual RAISE report, which at one point exceeded 100 pages in length. Much of the report was meaningless because the data had been broken down into numerous sub-groups comprising just a handful of pupils whose results would be compared to other groups, the cohort as a whole, and – most extraordinary of all – the national average. Small schools' RAISE reports were something to behold. With so few pupils, the possible percentage outcomes were extremely limited and data tables were filled with 0, 50 and 100% figures. Stripping out the statistical noise would leave very few useful pages; perhaps none at all. Ofsted would use the data to draw conclusions about school performance and challenge the leadership during inspection; and, of course, governors were expected to do the same.

Thankfully, RAISE is no more and Ofsted now produce an annual report known as the Inspection Data Summary Report (IDSR), which has undergone several revisions, slimming down from 22 pages in length in its first year of publication to 11 pages in 2018, and it is currently just 6 pages long. Schools should take note and strive for data minimalism, too. Governors do not need 100 pages of binary; instead, they need the following three summaries:

9.9.1 School demographics

Results without context are a blunt instrument. Certain factors – special needs, language, mobility, attendance, prior attainment, month of birth – can affect outcomes and it is strongly recommended that governors are provided with a one-page summary of school demographics to help frame conversations. Comparing the performance of one group to another is most likely misleading, but an awareness of the characteristics of cohorts can put performance into context and help anticipate future outcomes. In addition to a school-level summary, it is therefore advisable for governors to be given a breakdown of key contextual indicators for each year group. These might include:

- % SEND with breakdown to show number with an EHCP
- % pupils for whom English is an additional language
- % with low and high prior attainment
- % summer-born pupils
- % pupils eligible for Free School Meals
- % pupils who joined the school in normal joining year
- Attendance, including persistent absence.

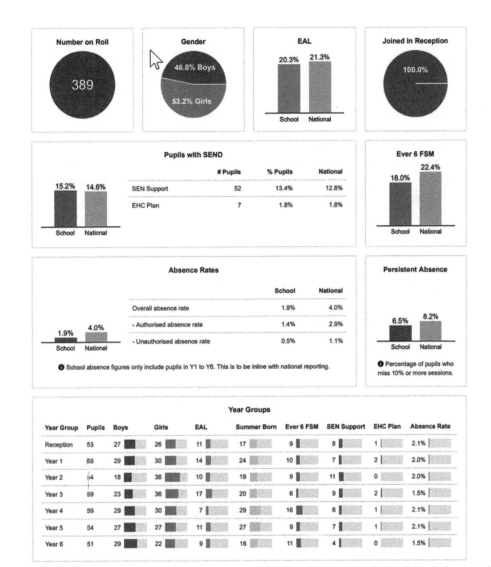

Figure 9.1. A simple, one-page demographics report for a primary school showing whole school data and a breakdown by year group.

Source: Insight.

9.9.2 Headline trends

These provide governors with a short report showing the headline results over the past three years compared to national averages.

In a primary school in England this will usually include:

- Percentage achieving a good level of development at the end of the Early Year Foundation Stage
- Percentage achieving expected standard in the phonics check
- Percentage achieving expected standards and greater depth in reading, writing and maths at Key Stage 1
- Percentage achieving expected and higher standards in reading, writing, maths, grammar, punctuation and spelling, and in combined subjects at Key Stage 2
- Progress scores at Key Stage 2 along with any significance indicators where applicable.

Secondary school headline data may include:

- Progress 8 score
- Attainment 8 score
- Percentage achieving grade 4 or above and grade 5 or above in English and maths
- Percentage entering EBacc and average score
- Average score (grade) in each subject.

The FFT Governor Dashboard is a good resource for data and trends at Key Stages 1, 2 and 4, but does not contain Early Years and phonics results. The Department for Education's Compare Schools website – the performance tables – contains data on Key Stages 2 and 4, including results over time, but does not cover other assessment points. Secondary school governors are well catered for by the FFT dashboard and performance tables, but primary schools should seek to create a simple report that presents results of all statutory assessments over the past three or more years.

Governors also require access to any Ofsted data report, which is currently the IDSR. This gives an Ofsted view of the school and is therefore essential reading.

A good tip when presenting results in the form of percentages is to express the gap from national average as a number of pupils. For example, a result that is

Figure 9.2. A section of a simple standards report showing the school's Key Stage 2 results over the last three years against national figures. Note the confidence intervals around the progress scores.

Source: Insight.

10 percentage points below national average equates to 10 pupils in a cohort of 100, 2 pupils in a cohort of 20, and does not represent a single child in a cohort of fewer than 10. This simple approach will help to make sense of gaps.

The desire to break results down and compare the performance of the various subgroups of pupils should be resisted for the reasons outlined earlier in this book. Groups are often small in number, their averages skewed by outliers, and they are not discrete – there is significant overlap between them. Gap data, therefore, is probably not telling you what you think it is, and this can result in kneejerk reactions and misplaced priorities. A case of not being able to see the trees for the wood. Awareness of the context of cohorts is vital, but issues are rarely as simple as relating to a specific group of pupils.

9.9.3 Current standards

Alongside a summary of demographics and headline results of previous years, we also need some information on the performance of current cohorts. In a primary school, this is quite simple and can be presented in a table on a single page that shows the percentage of pupils in each year group that are working below, within and above expectations in reading, writing and maths at key points in time. Those key points could be a previous statutory assessment such as Key Stage 1, the end of the previous year, and the current term. A further column showing targets may also be desirable, but it is worth referring to the section on targets earlier in this chapter first.

In a secondary school, with multiple subjects and possibly different approaches taken to assessment across key stages, reporting on current standards is likely to be less straightforward but simplicity should be sought. Presenting percentages of pupils in lower, middle and upper attainment bands is feasible, especially where informed by standardised tests, and this can be compared to prior attainment bandings based on the results of Key Stage 2 or 'on entry' tests. Alternatively, data showing the proportions working below, within and above expectations can be shown, and this may require grouping by set where relevant. At Key Stage 4, the focus is likely to shift towards predictions and how those compare to targets.

Taking context into account, governors should use this data to monitor standards over time, to check whether the proportions working at or above expectations are at least in line with baselines or targets and to see if there is consistency across subjects. There should be a particular focus on those working below expectations and conversations should centre on the types and effectiveness of the support provided to meet the needs of those pupils. There needs to be a recognition that data has its limitations, and it is at this point – when dealing with pupils that are struggling with their learning, have SEND or are causing concern – that narrative should take over from data. There are the headlines and there are individuals – there isn't really anything in between.

Year	Subject	Y2 Summer		2019-2020 Summer			2020-2021 Autumn		2020-2021 Summer		
		# pupils	% of pupils Expected or higher	% of pupils Expected or higher	Attainment Band Chart	Average Attainment	% of pupils Expected or higher	Attainment Band Chart	% of pupils Expected or higher	Attainment Band Chart	Average Attainment
Year 4	Reading	59	78%	90%	[bar chart]	100	85%	[bar chart]	88%	[bar chart]	100
	Writing	59	85%	88%	[bar chart]		88%	[bar chart]	85%	[bar chart]	
	Maths	59	75%	88%	[bar chart]	97	85%	[bar chart]	88%	[bar chart]	101
	Reading/Writing/Maths	59	56%	80%			66%		71%		
Year 5	Reading	54	63%	87%	[bar chart]	94	74%	[bar chart]	89%	[bar chart]	97
	Writing	54	67%	85%	[bar chart]		85%	[bar chart]	83%	[bar chart]	
	Maths	54	67%	80%	[bar chart]	99	80%	[bar chart]	89%	[bar chart]	97
	Reading/Writing/Maths	54	39%	65%			63%		70%		
Year 6	Reading	51	73%	75%	[bar chart]	96	76%	[bar chart]	82%	[bar chart]	100
	Writing	51	71%	80%	[bar chart]		84%	[bar chart]	82%	[bar chart]	
	Maths	51	76%	84%	[bar chart]	95	80%	[bar chart]	67%	[bar chart]	96
	Reading/Writing/Maths	51	43%	57%			63%		43%		

Figure 9.3. A suitable summary of current standards for school governors. The table shows percentages working at or above expectations at various points in time (Key Stage 1, end of previous year, autumn, and summer term of the current year). Bars show proportions working below, towards, within and above expectations. Numbers of pupils and average scores from standardised tests taken at the end of each year are also provided.

Source: Insight.

9.10 Reporting on the performance of groups of schools

Groups of schools, such as Multi-Academy Trusts (MATs), will want to report on the performance of their constituent schools to the executive board. This is a similar process to reporting to the governors of an individual school involving the same types of data. Simply present a table of percentages working at or above expectations – or on track for national standards or target grades – in each subject in each school alongside a contextual summary, which should, of course, include details of attendance. Presenting data from several assessment points is useful for monitoring standards over time in each school, and basing this data on standardised tests – the same tests administered at the same time under the same conditions – will reduce bias and ensure the results are comparable.

Dataproof Your School

9.11 Reporting to parents

Most schools have a statutory duty to report information on children's learning to parents and guardians on an annual basis. The Education (Pupil Information) (England) Regulations (2005) state that – in addition to a record of attendance, the results of any national tests, and the means by which parents can arrange a discussion with the teacher – the report must include:

- Brief particulars of achievements in all subjects and activities forming part of the school curriculum
- Comments on general progress.

Despite the use of the word 'brief', these regulations are often interpreted to mean that detailed prose is required, which results in primary school teachers writing a paragraph or more on each pupil's performance in every subject. Secondary teachers, meanwhile, will have to write statements for the hundreds of pupils they teach. And it is common for headteachers to contribute a comment for every child in the school. Reports can therefore extend to several pages and take weeks to prepare. But is this really necessary? Considering any urgent issues would have been communicated to parents at the time they arose, do lengthy written reports have any effect? Isn't the real value in dialogue between the parents and the teacher?

Many schools are seeking to address this issue and looking at ways to trim down reports so that they supply parents with useful information and meet the regulations whilst not adversely affecting teacher workload. With a bit of determination – and courage to break with old habits – annual reports to parents can be reduced to a single page, or possibly even postcard-size. Beyond the child's name, class and attendance record, a data-minimal primary school report could contain a single text box for the class teacher's general comments along with a table presenting attainment and effort grades in each subject. Secondary schools might take a similar approach with a tutor's general comment to accompany a table of attainment data – including results of any significant tests – and effort grades, which may be subdivided to indicate any discrepancies in the student's attitude to class and homework. Attainment and effort grades can be in the form of a number or letter.

It should be noted that some secondary schools have removed written reports altogether, in favour of tables of data that show, at a glance, where the main issues lie. The definitions of the various indicators act as 'comments on general progress'.

As with everything else, whatever approach a school takes to reporting to parents, that question – does it have impact? – is critical. If going above and beyond the requirements of the regulations is useful to all parties involved and has a clear impact on learning, then do it. Otherwise, do what is required to conform to the regulations and use parent consultations to celebrate achievement and discuss any concerns.

Box 9.2 — Case study: Cheshire Academies Trust

Over many years as a leader, I have seen first-hand the workload associated with producing an annual report. It was a voluminous task and one which teachers undertook meticulously knowing that they would be pored over by parents. As a school we valued the notion that they needed to be utterly bespoke but recognised that it would increase the workload significantly compared to schools who used standardised phrases. We abhorred copying and pasting because it depersonalised the report and parents would always know when they read it. However, with a focus on workload and its reduction to a manageable level, we examined how to reduce the information while retaining the meaning and personal nature. What we realised through talking to parents was that they simply didn't read the overview of what the children had covered. Rather they read and valued the teacher's comment far more. That was the bit they read to see how well the teacher knew their child.

With that in mind and spurred on by discussions about providing parents information in a more agile and frequent way, we decided to move to a termly report which was vastly slimmed down. It would include a bespoke teacher comment limited to one hundred and fifty words as well as results from across the curriculum. All of that would fit onto an A5 post card. We tracked the amount of time it took teachers to complete all of their comments and realised that, even if they completed a post card per term, it would still result in less time overall than the full annual report completed once a year. We mail merge assessment information straight from the Insight Tracking system and that again reduces teacher workload. Then the leadership produce, print and deliver all of the post cards back to teachers.

Parental feedback has been overwhelmingly positive. They receive a post card at the end of the term with parents' evenings sitting just after half term. This provides meaningful feedback to them every six to eight weeks. In summary, workload is down and communication to parents is up.

Steve Ellis, Chief Executive Officer, Cheshire Academies Trust

9.12 Summary

The primary purpose for collecting data is to inform audiences – teachers, senior leaders, governors, parents – about individual pupils' learning and standards across the school, or group of schools. In order to fulfil this vital function, data must be reliable, proportionate and unambiguous. Review current data collection procedures and always question why data is needed and what it will tell you. Strive for data minimalism by adhering to the old adage: if in doubt, leave it out. Be lightweight and nimble – carry only what is needed to get the job done. Reduce the information you report to governors and parents – consider the possibility that more data is not necessarily better and may in fact be counterproductive. Know the limitations of data – what it does and does not tell you – and do not attempt to make data prove something it cannot. Accept that comparing the performance of groups – especially small groups – is likely to be extremely misleading and result in misinformed priorities; and that often – particularly when it comes to pupils with SEND – there is no alternative to detailed, contextualised information on individuals. Simplify teacher assessment and free it from the distorting effects of performance management and progress measures; avoid reinventing levels with their inherent assumptions that there is some magic gradient that all pupils follow. Think about target setting: Do targets limit expectations? Are they achievable? Are they based on probability or an arbitrary flightpath that simply connects two points with a straight line? And finally, be honest. Data is essential to the successful running of a school and is a powerful resource, but it is easily manipulated and misappropriated. Collect what is needed to help teachers best support their pupils and to enable senior leaders to monitor standards, but always be mindful of the tensions this can create.

It is all about balance and this is hardwired into the culture of the dataproof school.

References

Benyohai, M. (2019) Banning GCSE grades before year 11 [Online]. Available at: https://medium.com/@mrbenyohai/banning-gcse-grades-before-year-11-8737b40180a (Accessed 7 May 2021).

Commission on Assessment without Levels (2015) *Commission on Assessment without Levels: Final Report* [Online]. Available at: https://assets.publishing.service.gov.uk/government/uploads/system/uploads/attachment_data/file/483058/Commission_on_Assessment_Without_Levels_-_report.pdf (Accessed 4 May 2021).

Independent Teacher Workload Review Group (2016) *Eliminating Unnecessary Workload Associated with Data Management* [Online]. Available at: https://assets.publishing.service.gov.uk/government/uploads/system/uploads/attachment_data/file/511258/Eliminating-unnecessary-workload-associated-with-data-management.pdf (Accessed 7 May 2021) (p. 5).

Newmark, B. (2017) *Why Target Grades Miss the Mark* [Online]. Available at: https://bennewmark.wordpress.com/2017/09/10/why-target-grades-miss-the-mark/ (Accessed 10 May 2021).

Ofsted (2021) *School Inspection Handbook* [Online]. Available at: www.gov.uk/government /publications/school-inspection-handbook-eif/school-inspection-handbook (Accessed 4 May 2021).

St Ralph Sherwin Catholic Multi Academy Trust and Northern, L. (2020) *A Framework for Assessment in Early Years, KS1 and KS2* (unpublished).

St Ralph Sherwin Catholic Multi Academy Trust and Northern, L. (2020) *A Framework for Assessment in KS3, KS4 (and KS5)* (unpublished).

The Education (Pupil Information) (England) Regulations (2005). Available at: www. legislation.gov.uk/uksi/2005/1437/made (Accessed 24 May 2021).

INDEX

A

accountability, 16–17
accountability frameworks, 4, 9, 70, 137–138
accountability systems, 21, 22, 32
adaptive tests, 49–50, 53, 64–65, 97–98, 105, 163
age, 33, 66, 70, 106, 117–118
    see also youngest children
age data, 34
age equivalent scores, 56–57, 123, 161
age standardised scores, 55–56, 161
age-related expectations, 158
Allen, R., 9, 24, 28
Analyse School Performance system (DfE), 125
Assessing and Monitoring Pupil Progress (EEF), 18
Assessing Pupil Progress (APP), 71, 124
assessment data, 141, 142, 145, 152, 154
  internal, 17, 18–19, 27–28, 113, 121–124, 136
  see also attainment data
assessment databases, 102, 114–115, 153–154
  benefits, 115–116
  content, 116–124
    contextual data, 117–119
    internal assessment data, 121–124
    prior attainment history, 119–121
  reports, 126–129
  see also school data ecosystem
assessments, 6–7, 11, 16–18, 45
  formative, 36
  pupils working well above curriculum expectations, 105–108

special educational needs and disabilities (SEND), 89–104, 162–163
  criteria-based assessment, 93–94
  engagement, 99–100
  gap analysis, 98–99
  group-level reporting, 95–96
  provision mapping, 100–104
  recording assessment, 91–93
  standardised assessment, 96–98, 99
  statutory, 16–17, 121, 125
  summative, 36
  see also standardised tests; teacher assessment
attainment data, 6–7, 12, 28, 32, 36–44
  bias, 37–38
  checklist, 43
  error, 38–40
  prior attainment history, 119–121
  reliability and validity, 40–41
  utility, 42–43
  see also assessment data
attendance, 7
attendance data, 35, 117
attitudes to learning, 8, 83

B

bar charts, 127
baseline assessments, 6–7, 61–63, 65, 120, 121
behaviour, 83
Benyohai, M., 159
best fit model, 80
Bew, P., 37
Bew Report, 80
bias, 18, 37–38, 74, 93
Bjørk, R., 72

Bramley, T., 81
Brilliant Club, 107

C

Carousel Learning, 132
Centre for Evaluation and
    Monitoring, 65
Cheshire Academy Trust, 170
Christodoulou, D., 18, 37, 93
Classical Test Theory, 40
cognitive ability tests (CATs), 50, 61, 106
Commission on Assessment without
    Levels, 17, 24, 112–113,
    153, 159
Common Data protocols, 141–143
comparative judgement, 81, 98, 122,
    131, 162
Compare Schools website (DfE), 166
composition, 79
confidence intervals, 50, 56, 59, 161
contextual data, 7, 12, 33–35
    assessment databases, 117–119
    checklist, 35
    Common Data protocols, 141, 142
contextual factors, 83
Covid-19, 147
Criterion-Based Assessment, 75, 80,
    93–94
current standards, 167–168
curriculum content, 72–73; see also
    national curriculum
curriculum expectations
    assessment and support for pupils
        working well above, 105–108
    assessment and support for pupils
        working well below, 89–104
    criteria-based assessment, 93–94
    engagement, 99–100
    gap analysis, 98–99

group-level reporting, 95–96
provision mapping, 100–204
recording assessment, 91–93
standardised assessment, 96–98, 99

D

data
    categories, 7, 12
    information provided by, 32–33
    purpose in schools, 16–18
    use in schools, 5–7, 9–10
    see also assessment data; attain-
        ment data; attendance data;
        tracking data
data analysis, 2, 6, 28, 143, 145–146
    assessment databases, 116
    gap analysis, 98–99
    question level analysis, 54–55, 64
data audit, 140–141
data literacy, 139, 146
data protocols, 141–143
data reporting
    to executive boards, 168
    to governors, 125–129, 163–168
    to parents, 129–130, 169–170
data strategies, 10–11
    checklist, 147–148
    need for, 136–137
    ten steps to creating, 137–147
Databusting for Schools (Selfridge),
    4, 40
dataproof philosophy, 150–151
dataproofing, 11–12, 32
    golden rules, 151–154
demographics, 164–165
Department of Education, 3, 6, 7, 18,
    21, 75–76
deprivation, 118
desirable difficulties, 72

development data, 7
Development Matters framework, 158
development over time, 8, 44–45
developmental experiences, 34–35
differential item functioning (DIF), 38
disadvantaged pupils, 118

E

Early Years education, 34, 158
Early Years Foundation Stage (EYFS)
    Profile, 75–76, 119–120, 158
Education (Pupil Information) (England)
    Regulation (2005), 169
Education Endowment Foundation
    (EEF), 3, 18, 61, 79, 107
Education Inspection Framework 2019
    (DfE), 9
educational progress, 44
Educational Reform Act 1988, 44
Ellis, S., 170
emerging writers, 78–79
engagement, 99–100
English as an additional language
    (EAL), 118
error, 38–40
estimates, 123
ethnicity, 34
executive boards, 19, 20, 168
expected progress, 21, 26; see also
    curriculum expectations
extended answers, 82–83
external pressures, 18–19

F

Fisher Family Trust (FFT), 105,
    123, 132
    Datalab, 5, 21
    Governor Dashboard, 166

formative assessment, 36
Free School Meals, 34, 98, 118
future results, 61

G

gap analysis, 98–99
GCSE assessment 37
        see also Key Stage 4
GCSE grades, 23, 105, 121, 126,
    155–156, 160
GL Assessment, 61, 65
Goldstein, H., 33
Goodhart's Law, 21, 36
Gove, M., 3
governors, 5, 20, 28, 125–129,
    163–168
group level data, 119
group level reporting, 95–96
group outcomes, 33
'Guide to the People Premium' (EEF), 3

H

handwriting, 79
Harford, S., 26
headline trends, 165–166
higher education, 107
How is data used in schools today?
    (FFT Datalab), 5–6
human bias, 37, 74
human error, 38–39

I

Improving Literacy in Key Stage 1
    (EEF), 79
Independent Teacher Workload Review
    Group, 151, 154, 159

individual learning objectives, 124
Inspection Data Summary Report
        (IDSR), 27, 164
Institute for Education Studies, US, 3
internal assessment data, 17, 18–19,
        27–28, 113, 121, 121–124, 136
internal pressures, 19–20
internal tests, 41, 48, 126, 160, 161–162

K

Key Stage 1, 37, 60, 120, 127, 168
Key Stage 2, 37, 60, 61, 80, 105,
        120–121, 166
Key Stage 3, 80, 89, 107, 126, 156,
        159–160
Key Stage 4, 107, 126, 160, 167
        see also GCSE assessment
knowledge, 82–83
Koretz, D., 51

L

languages, 34
learning, 71–72
    attitudes to, 8, 83
learning difficulties, 53, 63; see also
        special educational needs and
        disabilities (SEND)
learning-performance distinction, 72
Leckie, G., 33
levels, 21–22, 25, 112, 157

M

Making Data Work (Teacher Workload
        Advisory Group), 28, 114, 143
Management Information Systems
        (MIS), 131

measurement error, 39–40
medical experiences, 34
Messner, R., 150–151
Mind Matters (PLA), 75
mobility, 34, 117
mock examinations, 124

N

national curriculum, 70, 124
    emerging writers, 78
    levels, 21, 25, 112, 157
    written work, 80
New Group Reading Test (NGRT), 65
NFER, 61, 62, 65
No More Marking system, 98, 122, 162
normal distribution, 52
norm-referenced scores, 60
norm-referencing, 48, 51, 162
numerical progress, 44

O

objective-level tracking, 71–73
Ofqual, 80
Ofsted, 18, 25–28, 112, 113
    data collection, 154
    Inspection Data Summary Report
        (IDSR), 27, 164
    progress, 44
    School Inspection Handbook, 9
    special educational needs and
        disabilities (SEND), 95, 98
outliers, 53
    assessment and support for pupils
        working well above, 105–108
    assessment and support for pupils
        working well below, 89–104
    criteria-based assessment, 93–94

engagement, 99–100
gap analysis, 98–99
group-level reporting, 95–96
provision mapping, 100–104
recording assessment, 91–93
standardised assessment,
96–98, 99
see also special educational
needs and disabilities (SEND)

P

P Scales, 90, 99
parallel tests, 97, 163
parents, 129–130, 169–170
percentages, 48, 50–51
percentile rank, 57–58, 59, 61,
122–123
Percival, A., 71–73
performance, 71–72
performance management, 19–20,
28, 152
phonics, 120
Phonics Screening Check (PSC),
77–78
Potential Plus, 106
predicted results, 61, 155–156
Pre-School Learning Alliance
(PLA), 75
primary schools
Common Data protocols, 141–142
data reporting, 125–126
data reporting to governors, 166
data tracking, 6–7
performance management, 19–20
progress measures, 22–23
pupils working well above curriculum expectations, 106
reporting to parents, 169
standardised scores, 61

targets, 156
teacher assessment, 89, 158–159
prior attainment history, 119–121
progress *see* development over time;
educational progress; expected
progress
progress matrices, 126–127
progress measures, 21–24, 113,
152–153
special educational needs and disabilities (SEND), 90, 92
standardised tests as, 59–60, 62
Proprietary Question Level Analysis
(QLA) tools, 131
provision data, 7
provision mapping, 100–104, 132
pupil focus, 35
pupil groups, 27, 28, 33, 34
pupil mobility, 34, 117
Pupil Premium, 118
Pupils Requiring Support, 143

Q

question banks, 132
question level analysis, 54–55, 64

R

RAISE report, 27, 164
RAISEonline, 98
raw scores, 48, 49, 51–52, 53, 55, 56
reliability, 40–41
Renaissance Learning, 58, 65
reporting summary data
to executive boards, 168
to governors, 125–129, 163–168
to parents, 129–130, 169–170

Rising Stars, 58, 61
Rochford Review, 90

S

Sammons, P., 33
sampling, 51
sampling error, 40
scaled scores, 58–59
    difference between standardised
        scores and, 60–61
scatter plots, 122, 128
school data ecosystem, 131–132
school demographics, 164–165
school governors *see* governors
School Inspection Handbook (DfE),
    9, 44
Scottish Qualification Authority
    (SQA), 62
secondary schools
    Common Data protocols, 142–143
    data reporting, 126
    data reporting to governors, 166,
        167–168
    data tracking, 6–7
    performance management, 20
    progress measures, 23
    pupils working well above cur-
        riculum expectations, 107–108
    reporting to parents, 169
    teacher assessment, 159–160
secure fit model, 80
Selfridge, R., 3
setting, 107
Sims, S., 9
Soderstrom, N., 72
software systems, 24–25; *see also*
    school data ecosystem
special educational needs and disabilit-
    ies (SEND), 34, 45, 162–163

assessment and support, 89–104
    criteria-based assessment, 93–94
    engagement, 99–100
    gap analysis, 98–99
    group-level reporting, 95–96
    recording assessment, 91–93
    standardised assessment, 63–64,
        96–98, 99
assessment databases, 118
Common Data protocols, 143
provision mapping, 100–104
Spielman, A., 27, 98, 113
St Ralph Sherwin CMAT, 157
stakeholder audit, 138–139
stakeholder development, 143–144
stakeholders, 140; *see also* executive
    boards; governors; parents
standardisation of administration,
    49, 50
standardisation of items, 49
standardised scores, 49, 50–53, 122, 161
    adaptive tests, 65
    age standardised scores, 55–56
    difference between scaled scores
        and, 60–61
    percentile rank, 57
standardised tests, 20, 43, 160–161
    as baseline assessments, 61–62
    data produced by, 54–59; *see also*
        standardised scores
    devised by schools, 53–54
    downsides, 65–66
    main aspects, 49–50
    as progress measures, 59–60, 152
    pupils working well above cur-
        riculum expectations, 105–106
    reasons for using, 48–49
    special educational needs and
        disabilities (SEND), 63–64,
        96–98, 99
    suitability for young children, 62–63
    versus teacher assessment, 74

test selection, 63–64
    see also adaptive tests
Standards and Test Agency, 62, 99
stanines (standard nines), 58
Stanley Road Primary School, 71–73
Star Assessment, 65
statutory assessments, 16–17, 121, 125
streaming, 107
subject knowledge, 82–83
summary data reporting
    to executive boards, 168
    to governors, 125–129, 163–168
    to parents, 129–130, 169–170
summative assessment, 36, 89
Sutton Trust, 107

T

tables, 128–129
target setting, 132
targets, 123, 155–157
teacher assessment, 17–18, 70–71, 122
    accuracy and consistency of,
        83–84
    bias, 37, 38
    case study, 71–73
    contextual factors, 83
    emerging writers, 78–79
    how to simplify, 157–160
    primary schools, 89
    special educational needs and
        disabilities (SEND), 91
    versus standardised tests, 74
    and utility, 42–43
    writing well, 82
    written work, 79–81, 82–83
    youngest children, 75–78
    see also comparative judgement
teacher bias, 18, 37

Teacher Tapp, 5–6
Teacher Workload Advisory Group, 28,
    114, 124
Teacher Workload Survey 2016
    (DfE), 11
test bias, 37–38
test content, 59
test error, 38–39
test formats, 64
Testing Effect, 42
Tests *see* adaptive tests; cognitive
    ability tests (CATs); internal
    tests; parallel tests; standard-
    ised tests
Tidd, M., 60
tracking data, 112
tracking systems, 6, 24–25, 112–113
    assessment databases, 114–115,
        153–154
        benefits, 115–116
        content, 116–124
        purpose, 114–115
    see also school data ecosystem
transcription, 79
Treadaway, M., 21
Twist, L., 60

U

understanding, 82–83
utility, 42–43

V

validity, 40–41
value added, 21, 44, 61
Van der Vleuten, C.P.M., 42

Dataproof Your School

Venn diagrams, 129, 130
Vitello, S., 81

W

What Works Clearinghouse, 3
whole class feedback, 72
William, D., 8–9
Workload Reduction Toolkit (DfE), 11
writing well, 82

written assessments, 105
written work, 79–81, 82–83
    emerging writers, 78–79

Y

Young Gifted and Talented programme,
    106, 107
youngest children, 62–63, 75–78